Low Kicks

A comprehensive study of the Art of Realistic Kicking below the belt

Advanced Martial Arts Kicks for Attacking the Lower Gates

from Karate, Kung Fu, Krav Maga, Tae Kwon Do, MMA, Muay Thai, Capoeira and more

By

Marc De Bremaeker

D1710387

Fons Sapientiae Publishing

Low Kicks – Advanced Martial Arts Kicks for Attacking the Lower Gates. Third Edition. Published in 2016 by Fons Sapientiae Publishing, Cambridge, United Kingdom.

The First Edition was published in 2013.

ISBN: 978-0-9569907-7-8

Recommended reading, by the same author:
"Sacrifice Kicks - Flying, Hopping, Jumping and Suicide Kicks" (2016)
"Stealth Kicks - The Forgotten Art of Ghost Kicking" (2015)
"Ground Kicks - Advanced Martial Arts Kicks for Goundfighting" (2015)
"Stop Kicks - Jamming, Obstructing, Stopping, Impaling, Cutting and Preemptive Kicks" (2014)
"Plyo-Flex - Plyometrics and Flexibility Training for Explosive Martial Arts Kicks" (2013)
"The Essential Book of Martial Arts Kicks" (2010) by Tuttle Publishing
"Le Grand Livre des Coups de Pied" (2016) by Budo Edition (In French)
"i Calci nelle Arti Marziali" (2015) by Edizioni Mediterranee (In Italian)

DEDICATION

IN MEMORIAM

This book is dedicated to the loving memory of my father.

André Félix De Bremaeker

If I have seen further it is by standing on the shoulders of giants.
~Sir Isaac Newton

Dear Reader,

In this day and age, the life of a serious author has become quite difficult. The proliferation of books and the explosion of internet content has made it nearly impossible to promote work based on extensive research and requiring complex lay-out.
Please enjoy this book. Once you are finished, I would ask kindly that you take a few short minutes to give your honest opinion. A unbiased Amazon review, of even a few words only, would be highly appreciated and encouraging.

Thank You,

Marc

A good word is an easy obligation; but not to speak ill requires only our silence; which costs us nothing.
~John Tillotson

ACKNOWLEDGEMENTS

Without the active support of my wife and life companion, *Aviva Giveoni*, this book would not have come to life. Being an athlete in her own right, she understands the meaning of hard work and dedication.

Aviva

Among many teachers and heads and shoulders above, my late Sensei, -*Sidney (Shlomo) Faige*-, should be mentioned with longing thankfulness. Sensei Faige founded the Shi-Heun style of Karate.

Sensei Shlomo Faige

Special Thanks to my life-long friend and training partner, *Roy Faige*, for his help and support. Roy is now heading the Shi Heun school is also my co-author of *The Essential Book of Martial Arts Kicks*. His influence and advice is felt in nearly every page of this work and the previous books in the series.

Roy and Marc

Dotan De Bremaeker

Thank you to *Ziv Faige, Gil Faige, Shay Levy, Dotan De Bremaeker, Nimrod De Bremaeker and Itay Leibovitch* who helped by painstakingly posing for some of the photographs.

Most photographs have been taken by the author, by Roy Faige and by Aviva Giveoni. But special thanks have to be extended to talented *Grace Wong* for some long sessions. Thank you also to professional photographer *Guli Cohen*: some of the photographs in this book have been extracted from the photo sessions he gracefully did for previous volumes.

The drawings in this book are mine. Everything that I have learned about line art, I have done so from professional Illustrator *Shahar Navot*, who illustrated *The Essential Book of Martial Arts Kicks*. Thanks Shahar!

A lifetime of training for just ten seconds.
~Jesse Owens

Contents

FOREWORD TO THE "KICKS" SERIES

A goal is not always meant to be reached, it often serves simply as something to aim at.
~Bruce Lee

The 'Foreword' and 'General Introduction' are very similar to those of the previous book in the 'Kicks' series. In order to spare a near re-read to our faithful readers of 'Sacrifice Kicks', 'Stop Kicks', 'Ground Kicks' and 'Stealth Kicks', we invite you to go directly to the 'Introduction to Low Kicks' on page xx.

My Martial Arts career started with Judo at age 6. Judo was pretty new Fifty years ago, and a bit mystical in the Western World. A mysterious Oriental Art teaching how to use one's opponent's strength against him was a pretty attractive proposition for a wimpy kid. And the decorum and costume trappings made it a unique selling proposition. That is, until the Kung Fu craze of the Seventies, starring Bruce Lee, and then others.

In my opinion, what fascinated the Western masses, and the teen-ager I was then, was mostly the fantastic kicking maneuvers in the spectacular fights of those Kung-Fu movies. The bulk of the fight scenes were based on spectacular exchanges, the likes of which we had never seen before. What was new and revolutionary back then, may seem banal and common to today's younger reader. But we had been raised in the era of boxing and we had been conditioned by the fair-play of *Queensburry's* rules: we had no idea one could fight *like that*!

It was also the first time that the general public in Europe and America had seen a well-rounded Martial Art in action: punching, but also striking, kicking, throwing down, grappling, locking... It comprised all fighting disciplines in seamless aggregation. Wow! Judo was great, but I now wanted to *kick* like Bruce Lee. I therefore took up *Shotokan Karate*. 'Shotokan-ryu' is not the most impressive kicking style, but it was then the most developed Kicking Art outside of Asia and the only one available to me. It is as well and I certainly do not regret it. Though it is not an art known for extravagant kicks, Shotokan is very well organized didactically. It also emphasizes tradition, hard training, focus (*Zanshin*) and mastery of basic work. In all athletic endeavors, the continuous drilling of basic work at all levels of proficiency is the only real secret to success.

...And traditional Shotokan Karate drills and low training stances definitely fit this bill.

So, during the whole of my career, I kept practicing Shotokan Karate, or a Shotokan-derived style at all times. I also kept at Judo, my first love. But in parallel, I started to explore other Arts a few years at the time, as opportunities and geography allowed. During my long Martial Arts career, I also did practice assiduously Karatedo from the Kyokushinkai, Shotokai, Wadoryu and Sankukai schools. I also trained for long stints of TaeKwonDo, Muay Thai, Krav Maga, Capoeira, Savate-Boxe Française, two styles of traditional Ju-Jitsu and some soft styles of Kung Fu. This search is where I developed my individual methods and my own understanding of the Art of Kicking and its place in complex fighting. It also provided the basis on which to build my own personal research. Of course, this is strongly accented towards the type of maneuvers and training that favor my personal physiology and personality, but I have tried very hard to keep an open mind, among others through coaching.

Sometimes during this maybe too eclectic career, my travels took me to the **Shi-Heun** School of the late *Sensei Sidney Faige*, mentioned in the Acknowledgements. The *Shi-Heun* style is *Shotokan*-derived and mixed with *Judo* practice. It emphasizes extreme conditioning, total fighting under several realistic rules sets and the personal quest for what works best for oneself. And its self-defense training is based on no-nonsense *Krav Maga*. As this was only the early Eighties, this was definitely a prophetic ancestor of today's phenomena of Mixed Martial Arts of 'UFC' fame. The free-fighting rules in the *Dojo* were 'all-out' and 'to-the-ground', but this did not hinder the success of the School's students in more traditional tournaments under milder rules. The direct disciples of *Sensei Faige* did indeed roam the tournament scene undefeated for years.

Sensei Sidney Faige in action

In these days, points tournament fighting was mainly WUKO (World Union of Karate Organizations), with some notable exceptions like *Kyokushinkai* and *Semi-contact Karate* bouts. Unfortunately, WUKO generally (boringly) consisted in two competitors safely jumping up-and-down and waiting for the other to initiate a move, in order to stop-reverse-punch him to the body.

Sensei Faige with the winning Israeli National Team; the author and Roy Faige are on the right

When my name was called up in these events, there was usually some spontaneous applause from the spectators; they knew they were going to see, finally, some kicking. I apologize if it sounds like boasting; the point I am trying to make is that Karate fans of these times came to see kicking and rich fighting moves, and not some unrealistic form of boxing. And this is not to denigrate *Karatedo*, but more to criticize the castrating effect of unintelligent rules sets.

Marc and Roy facing off at the finals of a 1987 Points Tournament

Marc, kicking in point tournament

...It is my strong belief that Kicking is what made the Oriental Martial arts so appealing. As I have already mentioned in articles and previous books, I do firmly argue that *kicking is more effective than punching.* This usually causes many to stand up, disagree and maybe want to *punch* me, pun intended. This is an old debate, still raging, and I respectfully ask to be allowed to complete the sentence. I strongly believe that kicking is more effective than punching, **but proficiency takes much more time and work**. When presented this way, I do hope that this opinion is more acceptable to most. Let me detail my position briefly.

Kicking is more efficient than punching:

1. Because of the longer range

2. Because the muscles of the leg are much bigger and powerful than those of the arms

3. Because kicking targets, unlike punching targets, go from head all the way down to toes

4. Because kicks are less expected and therefore more surprising than punches, especially at shorter ranges

I readily admit that the opponents of my position do have valid arguments. They will

One needs to drill kicks from very close ranges as well

point out that kicks are inherently slower than punches and can be easily jammed because they start from longer ranges. They will also point out that kicking often opens the groin, while forgetting that so does punching usually as well. It is my experience that, - *after a lot of dedicated and intelligent work-,* many kicks can be *as swift as punches and can be delivered at all ranges and from all positions.*

...During all my training years, I invested a lot of time, personal drilling and original research into Kicking Arts from all over the world. I experimented with all training tips gathered and I endeavored to try all mastered new kick variations in actual free-fighting and competitive tournaments. Here is the place to note that this is *not* about a huge number of different techniques; it is about finding the best possible techniques suited to one's specific strength, physiology and affinities (Once you have found your **few** techniques and the best way to drill them, then you focus on a fast and perfect execution from all ranges and positions). During my quest in the realm of kicking, I slowly developed a personal kicking style based on my personal history and mindset. I researched most of the available literature, but very few treatises were actually *dedicated* to kicking. The few works I found about kicking were generally very good, but usually style-restricted and unorganized. I never found the kind of book that I would have liked to have at the start of my Martial arts career. And so I decided to write it myself and to share my global view of the subject. To the best of my knowledge, there has never been an attempt to compile and organize all the different Kick types and variation in such a way that it could serve as a reference work and the basis for exploration for the kick-lover. I did try to start this potentially huge work, probably imperfectly, with a series of Books I chose to name the 'Kicks Series'. A global overview of Basic Kicks was presented in **'The Essential Book of Martial Arts Kicks'** (Tuttle), translated in several foreign languages. Its success lead me to follow with the important lower gates attacks in **'Low Kicks'**, and then **'Stop Kicks'** about preempting, jamming, impaling, obstructing and 'cutting' Kicks. As a sign of these MMA times, the series was naturally enriched by **'Ground Kicks'**. Widely acclaimed **'Stealth Kicks'** then endeavored to cover misdirection and dissimulation while kicking. Later came **'Sacrifice Kicks'** rambling about Flying and Suicide Kicks. And we hope that all this work will be built upon by others in the future. As mentioned and underlined many times, kicking proficiency requires a lot of serious drilling. I have therefore also published a work about the basic general drills that will help you reach higher levels of proficiency. As in all athletic endeavors, it is the basic drills that will build the strong foundation needed; and it is to those basic drills that the truly good athlete will come back for further progress again and again. **'Plyo-Flex Training for Explosive Martial Arts Kicks and Other Performance Sports'** does present those general, basic but so-important exercises that one should regularly practice for continuous improvement of kicking proficiency.

And now last, but certainly not least: it is important to underline that my strong views do not try in any way or form to denigrate the Punching Arts. My personal philosophy is that Martial arts are a whole with a world of possible emphasis. A complete Martial artist should be proficient in punching, kicking, moving, throwing, grappling, evading and more. But every Artist will have his own preferences and particular skills in his own way to look at the Martial Arts as a whole.

...And here must I add the obvious: *there is no kicking mastery* without punching proficiency! Even for a dedicated kicker, punching will be needed for closing the gap, feinting, setting up a kick, following it up and much more... This will be made abundantly clear from most of the applications presented in this volume, just as it is clear from all my previous work.

It must be said that Punching is sometimes the best or the only answer in some situations. I have known and met some extraordinary Punching Artists using kicks only as feints or set-ups. On the other hand, great kickers like legendary *Bill 'Superfoot' Wallace* were extremely skilled punchers and working hard at it, as I personally experienced in a few seminars. Kick and Punch, Punch and Kick: well-rounded is the secret.

And this leads me naturally to my last point. I would not want my books and my views to be misunderstood as an appeal to always kick when fighting, and especially not as an appeal to always high-kick. The best kicker in the world should not execute a high Kick, *just because he can*. A Kick should only be delivered *because and when it is suitable* to a specific situation! Obvious maybe, but certainly worth reminding. In someone else's words:

Take things as they are. Punch when you have to punch. Kick when you have to kick.
~Bruce Lee

GENERAL INTRODUCTION: THE 'KICKS' SERIES

This book is not a "How to" book for the beginner, but, hopefully, a reference work for the experienced Martial Artist. It presupposes the knowledge of stances, footwork, and concepts of centerline, guards, distance, evasions and more. It also expects from the reader a good technical level in his chosen Martial style, including kicking. As this work is building upon the *Essential* basic level towards more sophisticated kicking maneuvers, all *Essential Kicks* are considered mastered from the author's point of view. The reader is invited to consult previous work already mentioned above. This book is intended as a tool for self-exploration and research about kicking outside experienced Artists' specific style. Therefore, the description of the different kicks is very short and typical examples are only briefly explained. The author relies more on photos and illustrations to exemplify his point. Let the reader try it and adapt it to his liking and morphology.

The author tends to prefer drawings over photographs to be able to underline salient points sometimes hidden in photos.

The experienced trainee will probably notice quickly that the basic background of the author is Japanese *Karate*. This cannot be avoided but was not deliberate. This book aspires to be as "style-less" as possible, as its purpose is to bridge across the different schools on the basis of common immutable principles. The author's philosophy is that Martial Arts are an interconnected whole, where styles are just interpretations of some principles and their adaptation to certain sets of strategies, rules, cultural constraints, or morphologies. It is one and same thing, although it may seem different from different angles. In the pictures and illustrations, the reader can see technical differences and adaptations from different styles. This is done on purpose to underscore the style-less philosophy of the treatise. Sometimes the foot of the standing leg is flat on the floor, as required in traditional Japanese styles, and sometimes the heel is up as in certain deliveries of Korean arts. It should be clear that the biomechanical principles are identical for trained artists and the small differences of emphasis are meaningless. It is more important for a trainee to adapt the technique to his morphology and preferences, once it is well mastered. This book definitely does not pretend to present an axiomatic way to kick! In the same vein, arms during kicking are sometimes close to the body in hermetic guard and sometimes loose and counterbalancing the kicking move. Hands can be open, or fists tight.

...Like in previous efforts, it has proved very difficult to name and organize the kicks into and within groups. The author has given the techniques descriptive names in English, whenever possible commonly used names. But the more complex, exotic and hybrid kicks have sometimes either several different appellations in use or none, while being difficult to describe. The names the author has chosen could certainly be disputed and improved upon by some. For the most basic kicks common to all styles, we have added the respective original foreign names. The author apologizes in advance to the purists of all styles: It is clear that the description of a technique cannot be in all details valid for all styles (For example, the basic Front Kick is taught differently in *Shotokan* karate than in *TaeKwonDo*). The original foreign names in Japanese, Korean, Chinese or Portuguese are just there as an indication for further research by the reader. It should also be noted that some techniques have different names in different schools of the same Art! For the more complex or exotic kicks, we have purposely omitted original names. Only when a kick is especially typical of a certain style, did we mention it, as a tribute to the specific school. The author also apologizes for his arbitrary transcription of foreign names, as purists could dispute the way it was done.

The kicks presented in this volume are tagged "Advanced". This does not necessarily mean that they are more difficult to execute than the *Essential* basic kicks. On the contrary. Besides being a requisite of some form of classification, it mainly means that the principles behind the "basic" kicks should be first thoroughly mastered. A *Front Stop Kick* is relatively easy to perform and slightly different than a regular Front Kick. But for maximum power, it is important to follow the same principles of a basic Front Kick, with chambering, kicking through and chamber back. And the principles of the leg development stay the same for the more difficult Flying Front Kick. And even if a Low Front kick seems easy to perform, it will be done so under the same principles already mastered for maximum speed and power. A typical Feint Kick, the Roundhouse-chambered Front Kick is slightly tricky to master, but it is more a question of hip flexibility and acquaintance drilling: the principles behind the power of what is ultimately a Front Kick stay the same. Once the principles behind the basic Front Kick are mastered, all other "Advanced" kicks will be faster and more powerful. **This is all about mastering the basics and principles first**, and only later trying out variations in all kinds of situations, fancier or not. This is, by the way, true for any other physical activity. But because Advanced Kicks are more a variation on the theme of their underlying basic kicks, they will be presented in all their complexity by many variations in specific applications.

This volume will not detail *Essential* basic kicks. If needed for the clarity of the narrative, some of them will be very briefly illustrated as a reminder. This volume deals with **kicks aiming for the lower gates** only, as a variation of all six basic categories of Essential Kicks presented in previous work (Front, Side, Back, Roundhouse, Hook and Crescent Kicks).

...Further volumes are in preparation to present the complex Multiple kicks, the devastating Joint kicks and the no-nonsense Self-Defense Kicks.

Some Advanced Kicks have been omitted, as the author felt he had to draw the line somewhere. Again the decision was arbitrary, and could be considered as open for discussion. First have been omitted the whole range of nuances of a given kicks: As already mentioned, the same basic kicks are delivered in slightly different ways in all different styles and schools. The small differences come from the different emphasis of each style, and do not alter the basic principles. The author therefore described the kicks in the way his own experience dictates as best, and each reader can adapt it to his own personality. Many possible variations are presented for completeness in the applications though. Secondly, hybrid kicks variations have been omitted, as the infinite number of intermediate possible deliveries in between two kicks would make this endeavor ridiculous. For example, many possible kicks as hybrids of Front and Roundhouse Kicks exist, each one with different levels of emphasis on the "front" side and the "roundhouse" side. In this specific book about Low Kicks of all types, it is even truer:  there are a great number of deliveries possibilities to execute a Low Front Kick, as will be presented in the text. Kicks combinations, and kick-punch combinations are infinite in numbers and will not be presented as such; *but hinted at in the Applications.* Knee strikes, although very effective and versatile when delivered low, will not be presented; for the purpose of this work, they will not be considered as kicks.

Flying Knee Strike

The remaining **'Low' Kicks** which will be presented in this work, will be so, generally, in a set descriptive way: After a brief **General** introduction and the **Description** of the kick (mainly by illustrations), the main **Key Points** to remember for a good execution will be noted. Please remember that the book is intended for conversant martial artists. The relevant **Targets** to be kicked in most applications will be mentioned, although only general targets will be mentioned: The specific and precise vulnerable points are out of the scope of this volume. Examples of **Typical Applications** will then be detailed and illustrated. The typical application will generally be, unless irrelevant, a detailed use or set up of the given kick in a tournament-type situation. This will generally be a movements combination based on alternating different attack angles or/and levels (For example: hi-lo-hi, or/and outside/inside/outside), or the Progressive Indirect Attack principle as it is called by *Jeet Kune Do* artists. The tactical principle involved will not be detailed or presented systematically though, as it is beyond the scope of this volume. Of course, those applications will also usually be relevant to real life situation, and training work.

...Whenever possible, *Specific Training* tips to improve the given kick will be detailed. The specific training section will be brief and will only deal with the very specific characteristics of the kick and the ways to perfect them; general kick training guidelines are outside the scope of this book. The training of a *Low Kick* is generally also the drilling of the corresponding Essential basic kick, before the eventual adaptation to its lower delivery. Back to basics then! Last, and in order to widen the scope of applications, additional examples of the use of the kick will be presented, generally more suitable to a *Self-defense* or Mixed Martial Arts application.

And now the reader is asked to remember that the fact that this particular book (and the whole 'Kicks' Series) has cataloged a great number of kicks does not mean that he has to know and master them all. As already mentioned, a good Martial Artist must first master the basics of his chosen style by hard work on the *Essential* techniques. Only when he has done so, should he try advanced maneuvers and special techniques from other Arts. He should then drill new and unconventional techniques, and then try them in free fighting. A real Artist will then know how to choose only *a few* techniques that are suitable to his morphology, psychology and liking. These very few techniques will then have to be drilled for thousands and thousands of times until they become natural. During the fight, it is the *body* that intuitively choses the best technique to be used. If you have to think about what to do, you have already lost! Practice makes perfect. Again, in other people'words:

I fear not the man who has practiced 10,000 kicks once, but I fear the man who has practiced one kick 10,000 times.
~ Bruce Lee

and:

Train hard, fight easy
~Alexander Suvorov

So drill the Kicks and Applications as presented. Then adapt them to your physiology and psychology. Keep drilling and try them in free fighting. The follow-up presented are indicative only and intended to make you think. Try them before replacing them by your own.

And now, let us go to LOW KICKS...

INTRODUCTION TO LOW KICKS

What counts is not necessarily the size of the dog in the fight - it's the size of the fight in the dog.
~Dwight D. Eisenhower

GENERAL

Low kicks are no doubt the most practical and effective kicks for self-defense. There are plenty of reasons for that:

- First and foremost, they are relatively **easy to master** and do not require outstanding flexibility, or even warming up for that matter.
- Low kicks are also very **fast**, as they start from close to their targets. They can be used from very close and with nearly no limitations.
- They also are **easy "not-to-telegraph"**: with some training, they can be lashed out with a completely immobile upper body (See *Stealth Kicks*).
- They also are very **difficult to block**: You cannot bend over to block them, as it would be suicidal, and evasion is generally the only viable countermeasure. Although you can sometimes block a low kick with your shin, or absorb the blow with a fleshy area of your leg, it is usually best to remove the target from the attack vector.
- But above all, the low kicks are extremely effective because of the **sensitivity of their natural targets**: the groin of course, but also the nerve-rich sides of the thighs, the knee from all sides,-definitely the most fragile joint of the body-, the painfully sensitive shins, the aptly-named Achilles' tendon, the ankles and the toes. The knee is an especially attractive target: because of its anatomical build, it is extremely vulnerable and can be dislocated with very little force from all angles: front, back and both sides. An opponent with a wounded knee will be both suffering and be practically immobilized. Bruce Lee used to underline the fact that a child had enough power to break a grown man's knee.

Low Kick in tournament
– Marc De Bremaeker

...It is therefore clear why Low Kicks would be the weapon of choice in a self-defense situation: formidable, especially from close up.

Many schools, mostly of non-sport Martial Arts, *do not kick above the belt*, on the basis of a simple risk/reward argument: Low kicks are very effective without the need to endanger you too much. For example: *Tai Chi Chuan*, *Wing Chun* and other soft styles of *Kung Fu*; some *Okinawan Karate* schools and many more. I personally do not support this approach, but it is a valid tactical choice, and it is also certainly true for some fighters with certain morphologies or personalities.

Although low kicks used to be forbidden in the *sport* applications of many Martial Arts, they are nowadays practiced and legitimized in more and more of the hardest of fighting arts. It must be underlined that their practice is extremely important for the complete Martial Artist, as training in a low kick-free environment will cause the development of bad habits and a false sense of security. In the real world, you should expect being kicked in the groin and shins!

I can illustrate this point with a personal anecdote: As a young successful but cocky non- and full-contact Karate fighter, I took up *Savate-Boxe Française* in Brussels in the late Seventies, to complement my training. My first fights were a disaster and did cut me fast to size: Every time I tried to attack, I was stopped in my tracks by painful "*Coups de pied bas*" (soccer-type low front kicks to the shins) to which I was not accustomed, as there was no low kicking in most types of Karate tournaments. It made me painfully aware of the fact that the way you train and spar, in any Martial Art, will cause you to adopt very specific habits, often veering you away from realistic fighting. [Another example, opposite in fact, of this is the inability of tough and fierce low-kicking *Kyokushinkai* fighters, to deal with straight punching to the face, which was forbidden by their competitive fighting rules]

Low kicks are an important integral part of any realistic Martial Arts: you must practice them, train just like for any other type of kicking, and spar in a setting where they are allowed. Only if you are aware that you can be low-kicked, will you learn to correctly gauge distance and the danger zone in relation to your opponent.

Stopping a Kick with a Low Kick: Soccer Low Front Stop Kick

TRAINING LOW KICKS

The fact that **Low Kicks** are relatively easy to learn and to deliver does not mean that you can avoid hard training and assiduous practice. Big mistake! You should treat those kicks just like all others: practice hard for speed, power, timing and a no-telltale delivery. Practice them in versatile combinations and as stop-kicks, use them as checking-up or attrition kicks. You must drill every aspect of these kicks,- just like with all other kicks-, until they become second nature. Most specific training drills are identical to those of the basic *Essential* Kick the low kick is derived from. And general drills for kick explosiveness are as relevant to low kicks as to regular and high kicks. The reader is invited to consult *"Plyo-Flex Training for Explosive Martial Arts Kicks"* for a basic training regimen built on scientific principles and based on the combination of **Plyometrics** and **Intense Stretching**.

There are, though, some common pointers in most low kicks-training methods.
You should train for power, just like high kicks, by hitting for example the long hanging heavy **bag**, a standing bag held by a partner, a lying bag or a tire hold by a partner. Use what will provide a more realistic "give" for the kick. A regular hanging bag is usually not very suitable for drilling kicks below the groin area. I personally like the old **tire** because of the penetrating "feel" you can get when kicking it.
Hit fast, powerfully, and an inch ***into*** the target; but remember that leg retraction is as important as with high kicks (unless it is a *Stomping Kick*). When you practice Low Kicks for power, always remember to also concentrate on a *stealthy* **un-telegraphed delivery**.

Drill Low Kicks on a lying bag

Drill on a bag held by a partner

Drill on an old tire

When training for Low Kicks, it is also important to remember that you will always be close to your opponent at delivery, and therefore your guard must be up! A good way to drill this into your head is to train with your hands tied up with a **belt** passing to the back of your neck. This way you train both high guard and un-telegraphed delivery.

Use a belt to tie your hands in guard; drill a no-telltales-delivery

→

As mentioned for power training, a very useful target for the practice of below-the-knee low kicks is the used **tire**, held by a partner. You can also use it lying down for stomping kicks.

The old tire held by a partner

The **medicine-ball** is of great use for practice: lying on the floor for ankle and lower shin kicks, and set on a lying heavy bag for knee-high kicks. You should kick the ball with a football/soccer mind: send the ball as far as possible! Of course, Kung Fu artists will also use the **Wooden Dummy** illustrated in the Photo.

Stomp on the old tire

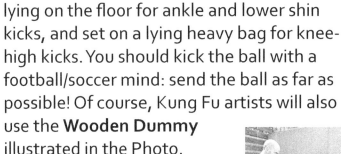

The use of the medicine ball for low kick practice

Wing Chung's Mook Jong; the Wooden Dummy

Train for accuracy on hanging **tennis balls**: You should have balls hanging at mid-shin, knee, mid-thigh and groin levels. Examples will be shown in the text.

But the most important exercise in low kicking training is **partner** sparring: use protective gear and work on your timing and speed against a moving opponent. Use **shin-guards** and striking pads, and always be very careful with the knee joint.

There are two more drills that I think are of the utmost importance, and that basically are about range and distance: You should train **1.** for the delivery of unexpected Low Kicks from the *outer* range, and **2.** for automatically low-kicking when you get to *clinching* range:

1. Train for low kicks from a **long-kicking range,** by using footwork only (shuffling, steps, angled steps, jumping,...).Only after having mastered this, should you start including feints or additional moves to help you close the gap: It is about the speed of the footwork first! Many examples will be scattered in the various applications presented.

Drill footwork; for example half-hop step before low kick

...
2. You should train for various suitable low kicks **in the clinching position**: Work with a partner and alternate. You should then train for getting into clinch and simultaneously kicking: It should become a second nature to you to automatically launch a low kick as soon as you get close to clinching.

Clinching should automatically bring up immediate low kicking

TO CHAMBER OR NOT TO CHAMBER?

In previous work (*The Essential Book of Martial Arts Kicks*), we have covered many basic kicks with an infinite array of variations, as we are trying to cover the whole realm of Martial Arts kicking in a style-less manner. Every kick usually has plenty of small possible variations, specific to some styles or schools, or simply more adapted to one's morphology or personality. Low Kicks are much less codified that the basic kicks of most Martial Arts, and there are more than one "correct" way to deliver them. One of the most significant personal inputs that can be introduced in the kick delivery is the amount of chambering. First as a rule of thumb, a low kick must only be chambered, at the maximum, to the point where natural leg extension brings the foot to the target. There is no point in chambering the knee to waist level in order to deliver a simple straight Front Kick to the ankle (unless it is a stomping kick). And some schools advocate even no chambering at all, arguing that the sensitivity of the targets makes the pursuit of maximum power by chambering, superfluous. I definitely say that this is up to you! Just remember the following and get to your own personal conclusion:
Maximum chambering will give you much more power, but will make your kick slower and easier to detect. It is a must, though, in most stomping kicks. And then, one kick could be enough to finish up a fight...

No chambering will make a surprisingly fast and indiscernible kick, but inherently less powerful. On the other hand, if it is successful, it will allow easily for more fast kicks to follow up, and maybe a full-chambered one at the end...

I personally think that the right answer is very much in the middle somewhere, like often in life. But I *also* believe that there is no "right" answer.

Low kicks are especially great as **Stop Kicks** or as **Counterattacks**. That is why they definitely star in our book about *Stop Kicks*. Being fast-reaching kicks, they can be

used to foil a developing attack or an attack on the verge of being launched. The Low Kick can target the opponent's front leg, or his stepping leg, or his kicking leg, and therefore so foil the attack while inflicting damage and pain. Several examples will be presented randomly in this book. Further text on the theory and applied practice of stop-kicking will be found in the book 'Stop Kicks', but many examples of the use of Low Kicks in stop-kicking will be presented here as well.

Low kick as a stop-kick to the standing leg by Roy Faige

Low Kicks are also great for counterattacks of all types: you are close to the opponent and have blocked or evaded his attacks, which puts him mentally or even physically, off-balance. Some typical examples will be presented in the book. A very typical example is the low-kick follow-up of a classical *Shorinji Kempo* evasion technique called "Hiki-Mi", where the midsection of the body is suddenly pulled back, just enough to evade an incoming kick or punch, with minimal move of guard or feet position. It is then very easy to low-kick the opponent as his kicking foot lands.

An example of Hiki-Mi evasion; opportunity for a low kick follow-up

Typical Shorinji-Kempo

Low Kicks are also *Stealth Kicks* par excellence. They happen far from the opponent's field of vision and aim at very low targets. It befalls the trainee to impart as much stealth as possible to his Low Kicks; and he is invited to refer to our book: 'Stealth Kicks - The Forgotten Art of Ghost-kicking'.

PRESENTATION

For the people who have read "*The Essential Book of Martial arts Kicks*" and/or "*Plyo-Flex Training for Explosive Martial arts Kicks*", the presentation of this book will be slightly different: there will be much less formal Description and Key Points, as *Low Kicks* are much less orthodox and codified than basic kicks. On the other hand, many more examples of Typical applications and/or Self-defense applications will be presented, as there are many variations of these kicks with special and specific uses; and it is important to present them for the completeness of this book. The Specific training tips will be more succinct, as a general overview of training methods has already been given in previous books.

We will keep presenting the kicks in the same chapter pattern though, for the sake of the internal logic of the book series, with more or less emphasis on the different subdivisions. The Presentation used here is, on the other hand, similar to that of the other works of the '**Kicks**' Series (*Stop Kicks, Ground Kicks, Stealth Kicks* and coming volumes).

Drill kicks with hands tied in guard: Low Side kick and High-chambered Front Stomp Kick

Low Roundhouse Kick to the inside knee – Shay Levy

A military operation involves deception. Even though you are competent, appear to be incompetent. Though effective, appear to be ineffective.
~Sun Tzu

THE KICKS

1. THE SOCCER LOW FRONT KICK

Gedan Geri (Karatedo), Coup de pied bas (Savate-Boxe Française), Teng Pai (KungFu), Oblique kick (Jeet Kune Do)

General

This is probably the most common rear-leg Low Kick. Fast, and punishingly directed to the shin, it is the kick of choice to gauge your opponent and harass him. But when the opportunity arises, it can become the full-powered kick, with no pulling-back rearwards, that can decide of a fight's outcome.
It is a very useful Stop Kick when directed at a raiding leg, and it can be delivered in a number of ways described later below.

In some karate tournaments, where low-kicking was forbidden, a variation of the kick was shamelessly used to attrite the opponent's legs, under the guise of a failed leg sweep.

Old Judo throws were coming from Ju-Jitsu and Chinese Kung Fu and were executed with full-fledged kicks

Similarly, in early Judo tournaments, there was much kicking to the legs in the guise of sweeps in order to "soften" the opponent. Both anecdotes will remind the fighter how efficient and ubiquitous this kick is; and that, if he has to sweep his opponent, he should do so with a kick in mind, just as it was done in old Ju-Jitsu!

The Soccer Kick connects with the inner side of the foot, which will be even more painful if you are wearing hard-soled shoes. For bare foot delivery, this gives the added advantage of not having to connect on the hard shin with the ball of the foot: Some people, for fear of hurting their toes, will instinctively kick slower when using the ball of the foot. Of course, this is where impact training is important: kicking the heavy bag, the tire, the *Makiwara*; one drill out the fear of hurting his feet and toes, and must train to deliver maximum power.

The kick is, of course, a natural kick in *clinch* position. It is great to use in between techniques to "soften" the opponent; see the Photos *at the top of next page* for a **softening** kick to the rear leg as a preparation for a knee strike to the ribs on the front side.

➡

Clinching maneuvers: Soccer kick to the rear shin; then knee to the ribs

The versatile soccer low front kick

Kicking while leaning back to evade a slap

No leaning back and attacking the knee

Description

The kick is very simply delivered, with no chambering, directly from its rear foot position, in a straight line towards the target, usually the mid-shin. The impact is with the *inner side of the foot*, just like for a kick on the **soccer ball.**

The first Figure shows the classic delivery of the kick, with the upper body leaning proportionally back when kicking. The amount of leaning back is, in fact, up to you and the circumstances, giving the added advantage of taking you away from an eventual stop-jab or counter to the head. But in any case, it is important to minimize telegraphing: The body does not move (and start leaning backwards) **before** the kicking foot has overtaken the front foot.

Great for self-defense: The leaning-back Soccer Low Front Kick

I personally advocate no leaning at all (See second Figure): just kick and *either* lower the leg back rearwards (fast), *or* lower it forwards and follow up.

Great for self-defense: The no-body-leaning Soccer Low Front Kick

...In **Savate-Boxe Française**, the kick is delivered slightly differently for extra-power. The distinction is as much a mental one than a physical one; very much like training for flying kicks while imagining an invisible step to climb on. The *Savate* kick, which in their way of competing is very much a bread-and-butter kick, is based on sending the hip forwards first, while the foot is stuck at the level of the front leg. This creates physically, but also in the fighter's mind, an accumulating reserve of energy, like a coiled spring. The foot is then suddenly released in a burst of forward power (See Illustration). In *Savate*, the body generally leans back to keep your head out of harm's way.

Savate's typical coiling of the **"coup de pied bas"**

The classic kicks described have the kicking foot chambering back rearwards. We will now describe variations in which the kicking foot lands *forward*. And what better forward landing is there than square on your opponent's foot? Landing on your opponent's foot, not only hurts, but also immobilizes him while getting his attention away from other attacks. The Photos and Figures below show such a kick, with the additional illustration of a good use of the extra-backwards-leaning. You lean forward to provoke your opponent into a jab that you will evade by leaning backwards **while kicking him**. Your upper body movements will make him totally blind to the incoming kick. You do not recoil the kick back, but land on the foot of his kicked leg. Your foot is naturally turned outwards and stays on his. You control his front hand while circular-elbowing him in the head (*Mawashi Empi Uchi- Karatedo*).

Evade high punch while kicking; stomp and follow up

The low Soccer Front Kick can often be followed by Stomp & Push

If you now **push** him back, he'll fall easily *while seriously hurting his ankle.*

➡️

Another variation of the forward landing is the **Scrape & Stomp**. This is not a Stomp Kick (presented further on in this book), but a forward kick, which, after connecting keeps contact with the shin while painfully scraping down, until the kicking foot lands on your opponent's foot. The following Photos show the *Scrape & Stomp* landing after a Soccer Low Front Kick in the clinching position. Remember that clinching is an immediate "must-low-kick" position, and in the case of the Soccer Front Kick, it is coming from the rear leg for power. After *scraping* his shin and landing *on* his foot, you can *push* him backwards for a nasty fall.

But remember: As soon as you get in a clinch, low-kick, lest you'll be painfully kicked first!

Clinch, Low-kick, Scrape, Stomp, Push

Key points

- Keep you guard up as you are close.
- Minimize upper body movements for "no tell-tales" delivery.
- Always chamber back fast: after you connect and kick "*through*" the shin, retract the leg backwards or land fast and forcefully forwards.
- The Kick looks simple but *must* be drilled constantly for maximum power delivery.

Targets

Shins, ankles, knees and thighs; all low targets from all sides.

Typical Applications

A few typical applications have already been described, like the "*feint-forward and evade-back*" or the *clinch*. Another typical use of this kick is as a "**cutting**" kick. A Cutting Kick is a timing attack to the *standing* leg of a kicker, usually the standing leg of a high kicker. In fact, this is probably the most common use of Low Kicks, as detailed also in our book about Stop Kicks (Cutting Kicks are, by definition, Stop Kicks). ➡️

… The first set of Photos show how the kick is used on the calf (or thigh) of a spin-back-kicking opponent, stopping him in mid-spin with his back open for a reverse punch to the kidney and a subsequent back-of-the-knee stomp. Cutting Kick, Stop Kick,… whatever.

The Illustration shows in turn a typical *Savate* technique in which a high Roundhouse is absorbed in the gloved hand and/or the shoulder, while you simultaneously "cut" the standing leg while strongly leaning back. Follow-up with a fast jab! The form depicted in the illustration is highly typical of *Savate*, a great historical French Martial Art with Oriental roots.

The low kick as a stop-kick against a Spin-back Hook Kick

Typical Savate **"Fouetté"** *(Roundhouse) cut by a low Soccer Kick*

Specific training

The few examples added here will generally be valid for most of the other Low Kicks coming in the book:

- As mentioned in the introduction: drill against a tire, a lying heavy bag, a standing heavy bag, or a medicine ball. The Medicine Ball can be held in place under the foot of a partner for better visualization.
- You can drill for power with an elastic band tied to the ankle. After 10 repetitions, release the band and deliver 10 more kicks to a bag with full unhindered power. Then drill the other leg, with the band first.
- Do not forget the all-important partner sparring with shin guards. Take turns to deliver the kick while trying to go as fast as possible while not telegraphing it. Your partner will try to evade if he sees the kick coming.

An illustration combining several training aids: Medicine Ball, elastic band, shin guards

Self defense

Just like the Photos in the first (General) section, the following Illustrations show a typical use of the back-leaning while kicking in a self-defense situation. As an aggressor attempts to slap you in the face, you lean back to evade the slap while low-kicking him. You can then lower the leg while keeping control of his slapping arm, and immediately kick him again with the other foot. You can follow-up with a full-hipped circular elbow strike, and then more…

Double Soccer low Kick after back-leaning evasion

The next Photos then show the use of the kick to the very sensitive inside shin in a clinch position from which you have to act fast. The inside shin is full of nerve ends and very sensitive. Soccer-front kick his inside shin, then switch legs and kick the other inside shin. Use the fact that you have in this manner "opened" his legs in order to deliver a shin-kick to the groin. Bend the leg and follow up with a side-knee strike to the ribs, tilt the foot as you come down with a foot stomp. Push him down and away, and follow up.

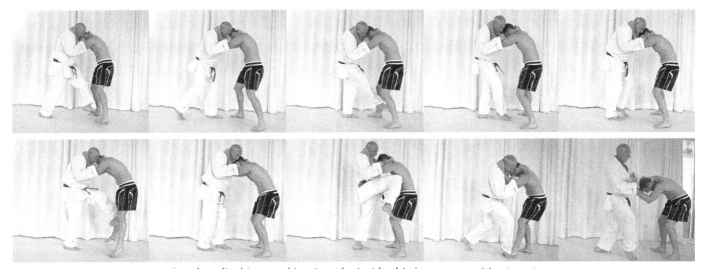

Another clinching combination; the inside shin is a very sensitive target

For our next example, the Photos at the top of next page do show an aggressive combination based on the *alternating of high and low attacks, as well as inside/outside angles.* If you can teach your body to intuitively execute these kind of combinations with alternating angles and heights, you will become a potent fighter. ➡️

… You confront your assailant and take the initiative with a *high* lunge/ reverse punch, covering up the delivery of a painful soccer *low* front kick. You lower the kicking leg forward to deliver a full rear-leg *high* roundhouse kick. Keep his front hand busy by attacking his face while lowering the Roundhouse-kicking leg forward. Keep control of his front arm while delivering another *low* Front Kick, eventually to his rear leg this time. In any case, do not stop your flow of attacks, preferably alternating high and low.

Alternate low and high attacks to confuse and hurt the opponent

There are, of course, an infinite number of variations of this basic combination. The next Photos show the same combination, *but* with a simple jab to start and a *rebounding* leg from high Roundhouse to low Soccer Front Kick. It is a purer version of the simple, but so efficient, hi/lo/hi/lo principle.

Two Soccer low Front Kicks in a simple but very efficient combination attack

The next Figures show the use of the kick as a "helper" for the success of an arm-lock against a knife attack. As you have succeeded in evading a direct knife attack to the body and controlling the knife arm, you pull it strongly to hyperextend while hitting the elbow. Deliver a Soccer Front Kick to his forward leg as a "softener" while you envelop his arm from above, eventually elbowing his chin on the way. Your Low Kick turns into a Stomp on the forward foot (This application requires some chambering) while completing the arm-lock. The stomping foot stays on the attacker's foot while you disarm him by seriously jerking his elbow. You can follow up by throwing him over your leg while elbowing him in the face, in a classic takedown.

The Low Soccer Kick as a "softening" maneuver to achieve a lock

And the Illustrations below show another way to go after evading the same attack in the same way. The "softening" principle we are trying to illustrate stays the same. This time, you pull his arm while getting control of his elbow with the other hand; all the while you deliver a regular (front-leg) low Front Kick to his front knee. You lower the leg, keep pulling, and deliver a Soccer Front Kick with your other (rear) leg to the same knee, getting into arm-lock position. Disarm him by jerking and push him to the floor.

Low kicks helping you to set up your arm-lock

Another great use of this kick in self-defense is against attempts to grab you at the lapels, shoulders or even throat. The Illustrations show how you retreat to put your assailant off-balance, while getting control of his arms. This is done in the Ju-jitsu or Aikido spirit of letting him rushing an open door. Your "retreating"-leg rebounds on the floor to come back to his forward leg in a Soccer Front Kick. In this position, you can follow-up by throwing him with a classic ankle block (*Sasae Tsuri Komi Ashi – Judo*); the Low Kick is then part of the throw, the way in was done in traditional *Ju Jitsu*: Kick, not sweep!

The Low Soccer Kick in a Judo throw

THE SOCCER LOW FRONT KICK

If your assailant has already grabbed you and your rearwards move does not put him off-balance, hit both his forearms from above with hammer-fist or knife-hand downward strikes, while delivering a fully powered Soccer Front Kick to his shin/knee (as Illustrated). Follow up with a knee strike to the groin or ribs, while keeping control of both his arms; no need to lower the foot in-between. You can then deliver a circular elbow strike to his head. A natural follow-up would be a neck-holding Hip Wheel Throw to send him to the floor (*Koshi Guruma – Judo*).

A low Soccer Kick will help you soften your opponent for a grab release

It is already clear to the reader that this kick is really an all-purpose weapon for self-defense situations. It should be used automatically in any situation where you are surprised. The *first* set of Illustrations show how to kick while leaning back and blocking or smothering a surprising fist attack. The kicking leg is lowered back in a big step to get you away from the assailant while turning back to stop him with a short back kick to the ribs. Under the same principle, you can deliver an annoying low kick, look like you are moving away but come back with a Side Kick as illustrated in the *second* set, of Photos this time.

Kick, retreat, surprise Back Kick

Low-kick; retreat; come back with Side Kick

The first set of Photos shows, again, an application coming from the older *Judo*, when it was still close to its realistic *Ju-Jitsu* ancestor. The Low Kick is used to block the knee of an assailant, resulting in a throw. It is similar to the milder *Hiza Guruma* throw of contemporary *Judo*, but with a full kick and a side throw. The second set of Photos

shows an application of this technique: As your assailant throws himself into a front-leg Roundhouse or knee attack, you evade forward to the inside, grab him and **kick** his standing knee or shin while pulling him down.

The kicking version of old Judo's **Hiza guruma**

Hiza-Guruma-*type* **kick** *while rolling inside a Roundhouse Kick*

The next Illustrations show another use of the Kick as a "help" to takedown and lock an opponent. This is not a sweep but a real **kick** to the shin which purpose is to hurt the assailant, to place him more off-balance and to "help" his standing leg into the "right" direction. As your assailant kicks you, you block and scoop his leg on the inside, and then deliver the Soccer Low Front Kick to his standing leg while lifting and circling his knee. Once he is on the ground, you join hands to start a Hip-Lock maneuver. Kick him in the *groin* while stepping over his leg. Keep pivoting (You can even stomp his head or spine while passing the leg over his body). Lock his hip <u>very carefully in training</u>; this is a very dangerous lock.

The Low Soccer Front Kick will help you set up the takedown and lock with less resistance

And we can cap this section with an example of an overall versatile simple *offensive* combination, presented in the Photos below. You start with a Low Soccer Front Kick to your opponent's front shin and let your foot rebound from his shin into a regular full Front Kick chamber. You deliver,-from this chamber-, a classic *Essential* Penetrating Front Kick to his groin, ribs or solar plexus. (Just to be clear: without lowering the foot back to the floor!)You chamber back and,- again without lowering your foot-, sweep his now-weakened front leg from the outside. Follow up with a high hand attack, like a palm strike. This whole combination works well because it is fast and nimble, because the sweep attacks a leg the opponent will be naturally releasing from body weight, and because the follow-up comes as you are on his blind side. In the case of a self-defense situation, the Front Kick becomes a fast Upward *Groin* Kick that blends naturally with the preceding Low Kick. The Low Kick, by the way, could be also a natural classic Front Low Kick, *as presented in the next section*.

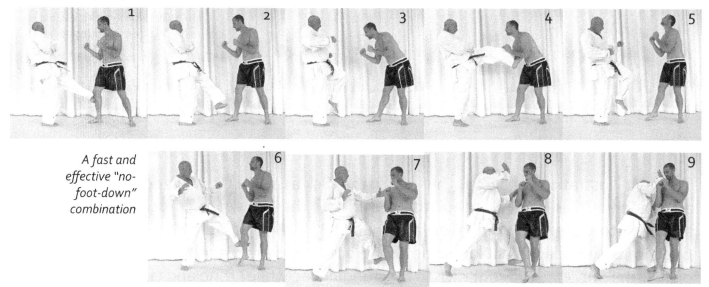

A fast and effective "no-foot-down" combination

Addendum

As already mentioned, low Kicks in general, and the Low Soccer Front Kick in particular, lend themselves particularly well to **stop-kicking**: they are fast, stealthy and effective. Many examples are presented in our book about *Stop Kicks*, and we are just giving a very simple one here to whet the reader's appetite. The Soccer Low Front Kick is the best maneuver to intercept and block a Front Kick in its early development. See Illustration.

The Soccer Low Front Kick as a Stop Kick or a Leg Block.

2. THE FRONT LOW KICK

Teep Robgaun (Muay Thai), Gedan Mae Geri (Karatedo)

General

This is simply the low version of the *Essential* basic Penetrating Front Kick. *Some* chambering is needed for this kick to be effective, but, -as already explained in the introduction-, the amount of chambering is up to you and the situation. This is a very fast kick, and very efficient in self-defense situations, especially if you have **hard soled shoes** on. Hitting a shin or knee with the hard tip of a shoe is extremely painful. If bare footed, you will hit with the ball or the plant of the foot, like for the regular (higher) Front Kick.

The Front Low Kick is great as a stop-kick

The Kick is very useful as a Stop Kick, as will be illustrated further on (See Photo). It can also be useful as a hard take-down (See second Photo)

Low Front Kick as a take-down

This kick is generally a rear-leg kick; but it can also be delivered with the front leg, especially in stop-kick variations, as will be shown in the applications. It is, again, a natural kick for very close combat situations like the clinch (See third Photo).

Low Front Kick to the rear shin in a clinch

Description and variations

The Illustration below shows the classic delivery: you lift the knee to the point where the natural extension of the leg will bring the ball of the foot to target. Some chambering is needed for this kick, but do not overtake this maximum. It would be totally unnecessary. This is clearly shown in the Illustration, and the reader is invited to compare it to the Illustrations of the next section, with the same kick, but delivered to *groin* level (The principle is the same, but the higher target requires a slightly higher chamber)

Chamber knee just as necessary, not more

A typical application of the kick, -and one that should be practiced even if only as a speed, flexibility and chambering drill-, is presented in the Figures below. It is a simple variation of the combo presented in the previous section, in which the Soccer Low Front Kick is now replaced by a regular Low Front Kick. The Low Kick, whether soccer- or regular-, is a *feint* and a *painful* distraction, as the foot "rebounds" on the shin to turn into a second Penetrating Front Kick to the body. In this example: As your opponent jabs, you lean back while controlling his hand and delivering the Low Front Kick to his forward shin. You immediately chamber back and, without lowering your foot, deliver a penetrating Front Kick to his exposed ribs (This is a Double Kick to be drilled a lot even if only for general speed and kicking excellence). You can follow up by hitting his face with a palm strike, while landing and keeping control of his arm. You can then sweep him. This kind of combination makes you understand how important to drill Low Kicks, so as to be able to deliver tremendous force with no special effort.

A versatile double kick starting with the Low Front!

Of course, like the previous kick, the Low Front Kick can be used as a "**cutting**" Kick. Just as a reminder: the *Cutting Kick* attacks the standing leg of a kicking opponent. The Photos series shows such a kick after you have blocked and taken control of his own Front Kick. Obviously, the principle is identical to that of the previous and related Soccer Low Front Kick (as is Illustrated in the last Photo).

Block the kick and low-kick the shin of the standing leg

The technique is nearly identical to the Soccer low Front Kick version

The Illustrations below show the use of the kick in a devastatingly aggressive combination against an opponent that you already control in a front headlock (*Guillotine*). This may seem overly crude to some artists, but it is the bread-and-butter of MMA fights. As soon as you have taken control of your opponent in the headlock, you deliver a first Low Front Kick to his shin, causing him to pull back his leg and hips. His retreating and pulling the leg back will cause him to be even more choked and vulnerable. You plant back your kicking foot far rearwards, in order to have room and momentum for a knee strike to his immobilized head. You immediately deliver a Low Front Kick to his other shin, keeping a tight headlock, and then a surprising flying knee strike! Keep at it until he surrenders. This could be considered a peculiar **lo/hi/lo/hi** combination, and, in any case, will do a lot to sap your opponent's will to fight back.

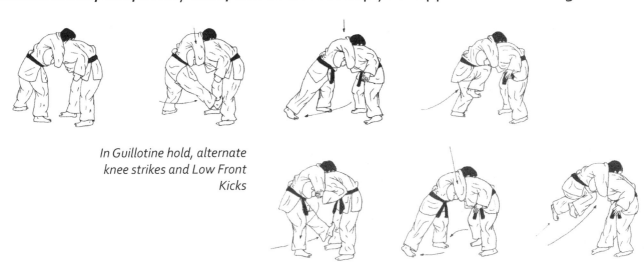

In Guillotine hold, alternate knee strikes and Low Front Kicks

The following Photos show a fantastic little *one-two* close-combat **combination** and a **must-practice drill**: Kick his front shin, and then hop to switch legs **fast and airborne** in order to hit his second shin with your other leg. Follow up. As a technique, it is very simple but also very effective when mastered. As a drill, it is great for speed and it has serious Plyometric attributes.

One/Two; switch legs airborne for a fast double low kick

The combination works regardless of which leg is forward

Description and variations (Continued)

Another interesting use for this kick is **counter-attacking,** as mentioned in the Introduction. The following Photos show how you retreat *just enough* to evade a body Front Kick, and then kick the shin of his landing leg. You can connect with the ball of the foot, or, -in a more stomping move-, with the whole plant of the foot. You can then follow up, for example with a high Roundhouse Kick from your other leg.

Evade back and kick the shin of the landing leg; connect with ball or plant of the foot

An interesting variation of this kick is the **low** version of the Essential *Outward-tilted Front Kick*. This allows you to attack the in-side of his front knee, but with the same principles of low chambering and fast kicking (See Photo).
The regular basic Outward-tilted Front Kick is illustrated at the end of the section, for information.

The low Outward-tilted Front Kick

An important variation of this kick, which we could have presented separately (but did not), is an **inside thigh kick** connecting with the **shin**. This technique is excellent when you get close to your opponent, whether on purpose by footwork or randomly as the fight takes you there. The Illustrations, at the top of next page, show how you step aside while getting control of the back of his neck and pull him both downwards and forwards. Kick the inside of his rear thigh with your shin and then forcefully chamber back while pivoting. You can follow up by pulling him to the ground while pushing on the back of his neck, or, as illustrated, by roundhouse-kicking him in the face.

$\longrightarrow$

*Low Front **Shin** Kick to the inside thigh*

The next Figures will show a self-defense application of this *Shin Kick* variation, aiming for the **groin** this time, in the dire situation where you have a gun hold to your back. If the gun touches your back and there is no danger of a stray bullet hurting innocent people while you deflect it, you can pivot in place and sweep the gun out of range, encircling the armed hand and delivering a circular elbow strike to the head. The **shin-groin kick** flows naturally into the movement and you can then catch the barrel of the gun, release his grip while breaking his trigger finger, and hit him in the head with the gun itself, in a classic *Krav Maga* series.

In a self-defense situation, go straight for the groin

 3

 4

 5

 6

Targets

Shins, knee, thighs (as illustrated here) and groin. Upper body if you opponent is bent-over or kneeling, as described in the *Self-defense* section below.

Low Front Kick to the rear thigh of the opponent

Key points

- Keep your guard up.
- Always chamber to some extent, this is a Front Kick.
- Always recoil forcefully, whatever the follow-up.
- Kick **into** the target, a few inches.

Typical Applications

On top of the applications presented in the kick's *Description*, we should also mention the **front-leg** version of the kick.

Low-Stop Kicks are usually better delivered as fast front-leg kicks. Much is said in our book about Stop Kicks, and we shall only hint at the subject here. The Photos describe what could be more aptly named as an *Obstruction Kick*. It is a more "pushing" version

of the Front Kick, used to **stop** the beginning of a move by your opponent, regardless of its type: footwork, kick, punch. By delivering the kick above the knee you stop any forward movement. You can follow up by immediately jabbing, and then kick again. This very useful kick is much used by *Muay-Thai* fighters (also at mid-section level) and called a "*Teep*" Kick.

Obstruction kick; just above the knee or a bit higher

The following Photos show an application of this *front-leg obstruction* version of the Kick: As your opponent shows signs of initiating an attack, kick/push into his front thigh to stop him. You so preempt his attack and confuse his plans. Follow up with a two-leg tackle, for example.

Teep *kick to the front leg as a preparation for a legs shoot*

Specific training

- Among all the drills already mentioned in the text, you should specifically train the **stop-kick** version of the kick and the "**double**" front kick version.
- You should also go back to the basics and drill the **basic** Essential Penetrating Front Kick.
- Note that the Front Low Kick should be sometimes drilled **with shoes on**!
- Low Kicks may seem easy but require serious training for **power** development: kick the heavy bag and the old tire to learn to kick fast and powerfully into the target.

Self defense

The Illustrations below show the use of the kick against an assailant attempting to choke you. Of course, you have to react as early as possible, before he even gets close enough to grab you. Lean back while front-kicking his shin, and *immediately* follow up with a groin kick and low straight-leg Roundhouse.

Stop the assailant in his tracks with a Low Front Kick

The next Photos show the use of the kick on an opponent that you have thrown to the ground or forced to kneel. This does not look very fair-play, but it is totally legitimate in a self-defense situation or in a MMA match where the rules allow for it. Targets to aim for are the face, the front shoulders and the ribs. (In these cases, you can also connect with the top of the foot). Remember to always kick **into** the target!

Kicking a downed opponent and follow-up

Kicking a downed opponent in the ribs

To conclude this section, we are giving an example of a kicking **take-down** using the Low Front Kick. Again, this technique could be a milder sweep, but, in our case, it is a fully-powered *Kick* which happens to have the side effect of throwing the opponent to the ground. The kick could also be a Low Soccer Front Kick, but in this specific application, it is a regular Low Front Kick and contact is made with the ankle when kicking. The Illustrations show clearly the reverse catching Block against a full-stepped Lunge Punch. Strike his face while pulling his caught arm forward and while repositioning yourself to his closer out-side. Kick *through* his front ankle towards his rear out-side while pulling his body forward to his in-side. He will fall on his face with a bruised lower leg. Follow up.

Kicking take-down; simple but effective

Illustrative Photos

The Essential mid-level Penetrating Front Kick

The Essential mid-level Outward-tilted Front Kick

Addendum

There is a variation of the Low Front Kick that we did not mention in previous editions, but should have. It is a very specific Self-defense version, best executed when wearing hard sole shoes, and in the spirit of the 'Scrape and Stomp' already encountered. **The Scrape-up Low Front Kick** aims at the lower shin and then scrapes up and into the shin all the way to the knee. It may seem simplistic, but the shin being very rich in nerve-endings, it is extremely painful. The kick is only relevant for close-up situations, but whenever possible, it is worth using. Make sure you kick forward as well as up, to scrape deeply.

The Shin Scrape-up Low Front Kick

And to remind the reader of the importance of the Low Front Kick in **stop-kicking**, here comes an example from our *Stop Kicks* book.

Stomping preemptive Low Front Stop Kick and follow-up

It is obvious that kicks to the lower limbs can also be delivered from the ground, and this is discussed and illustrated in detail in our book *Ground Kicks*. But we have chosen to extract from this book an example of a **Standing-up Kick**.

Going down will help the wrist-lock and the grab release; going up will help the power of the kick

Low Kicks are **Stealth Kicks** par excellence. The trainee should try to impart as much stealth as possible into his kicks in general, and in his low kicks in particular. We present here an example of the way the Low Front Kick is drilled in some Southern Kung Fu styles, where it is very much 'bread and butter'. The Kick is simply executed from the front-leg and as stealthily as possible: the rear foot glides behind the front for a hidden half-step, the hands stay high to keep the opponent attention and the head stays at the same height to dissimulate any movement. The front foot explodes forward as fast as possible to the opponents shin, preferably to connect just below the kneecap for maximum damage. This type of kick has several appellations, all of them referring to ghosts, shadows or the absence of shadow. Stealth indeed.

The Ghost Low Front Kick

As a last example, we are going to remind the reader that nearly all the variations of the basic *Essential* Front Kick can be adapted to low-kicking. The Illustration below shows how to attack the sensitive side of the opponent's knee from the front: simply with the **Outside-tilted version** of the Low Front Kick!

3. THE GROIN FRONT KICK

Kin Geri (Karatedo)

General

The *Upward Front Kick* and the *Straight-leg Upward Front Kick* are basic *Essential* Kicks, presented in previous work. We present here the exclusive **groin kick** emphasis for these kicks because of their central use in realistic fighting and self-defense situations. There is no need to further comment on the importance of the groin as a target, as exemplified in the *Krav Maga* series below.

The kicks described here are exactly the same as the basic Essential Front Kicks mentioned, but exclusively targeting the groin. Other Essential Kicks are especially suited for groin kicking, like the *Lift Kick* and the *Phantom Groin Kick*; the reader is

invited to refer to further reading to complete his groin kicks array.

The redoubtable Groin Front Kick as a counter

*Classic **Krav Maga** series: Release from a hair grab with the groin kick as a mellowing strike*

*Classic **Krav Maga** series: Double wrist grab release with groin kick as a finishing blow*

Description

The groin kick needs not be especially powerful: Speed and no-telegraphing are much more important qualities. The kick can be delivered with the rear leg, or with the front leg, statically or with hopping, or after some other footwork. Some chambering is needed but, again, not more than needed to complete trajectory, as illustrated the Figure. Connect with the top of the foot and/or the ankle.

The next Illustration, below, shows a **forward hopping** *front-leg* delivery of the same kick.

Rear-leg *Front Groin Kick; chamber knee just as much as needed, not more*

Front-leg *Groin Kick*

Key points

- Chamber back forcefully: Snap back and do not leave your foot around. The *whipping* effect adds damage to the groin area.
- But remember to kick *into* the target, not slap on the surface.
- Either feint towards his face to keep his attention up, or keep the upper body totally immobile to avoid telegraphing the kick.

Typical Applications

The Photos below show a typical basic *Sankukai Karate* application. The *Sankukai* style of Karate was founded by the Japanese champion *Yoshinao Nanbu* and is very popular in France where he settled down. It is a dynamic style strongly based on evasions and circular kicking techniques. The application presented is a basic codified exercise taught to students as *"Ippon Kumite Godan"*, and also found in their basic *Randori Ni no Kata*: A Penetrating Front Kick is evaded sideways (in-side) to allow for a nearly-simultaneous rear-leg Groin Kick, as the opponent's leg is still airborne. In the less sophisticated preparatory exercise described in the first Photos of this section (above, P 46), the evasion is made safer with a block and a catch; but note that the opponent's leg is released *during* the execution of the groin kick to allow the opponent's body to "fall" onto the rising kick.

Groin Kick while evading a Front Kick without blocking it; speed is of the essence

The next Photos show an application of the kick against a frequent user of Spin-back Hook Kicks. In this example, you evade his preparatory Low Kick by lifting your front leg, and then crouch down while he spins back to let his high Hook Kick fly over your bent body. Crouch as much as your style or physiology would allow: A *Capoeirista* would get very low and use his hands to rebound. Straighten up as soon as the kick has passed you over and kick him in the groin while he lands his foot. You can also jab his face simultaneously for good measure.

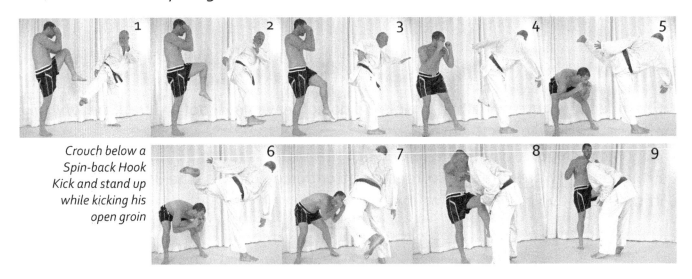

Crouch below a Spin-back Hook Kick and stand up while kicking his open groin

Specific training

Drill for speed on a heavy bag hanging with its bottom at groin level. Strive to deliver the kick with no tell-tales and from different distances.

Self defense

The Illustrations below describe a very efficient self-defense technique that can be used each time you find yourself on the blind side of an assailant. Evade a straight attack on your opponent's out-side and control his front arm. Pivot to deliver an Upward Front Kick with the top of the ankle or even the shin into his groin *from behind*. Only then, release his front arm and bend down to get hold of both his ankles that you will pull back and up while striking his lower back with the top of your head. This will cause him to fall hard forward. As you hold both legs open, you can kick the groin, again, as he falls! You can then follow up with many techniques: We have shown here a Stomp Kick to the ankle to neutralize him, but you could deliver a Flying Stomp, or you could jump on his back if you are a good submission-groundfighter.

The redoubtable groin kick from behind

3 4 5 6

Illustrative Photos

The Essential Upward Front Kick

The Essential Straight-leg Upward Front Kick

The Essential Front Lift Kick

The Essential Front Groin Ghost Kick

Vintage Low Front Kick in tournament – **Roy Faige**

Addendum

As already mentioned many times, Low Kicks are great **Stop Kicks**. The self-evident stopping power of a groin kick must not be explained. As illustrated by several examples above, the Groin Stop Kick is especially indicated against a kicking opponent. In this additional example, extracted from *Stop Kicks* and presented at the top of next page, you use the Groin Front Kick against an assailant fond of Spin-back Hook Kicks. Kick fast with the front leg as he spins and lifts his leg to really offer his groin. You are basically groin-kicking from behind, and you could 'hook' into his groin for further damage as explained later in this subsection. As he lands, you could catch his shoulder and sweep him. An Axe Kick would end the confrontation.

Front-leg Timing Stop Kick to the groin; note the partial retreat into Cat Stance

A variation of the kick that we did omit from the First Edition, is the Leaning-back Groin Front Kick, often found in Southern Kung Fu styles. It is easy, fast and has the advantage of removing your head from the counter danger zone. It is also very devious in a way underlined in our book about Stealth Kicks: the leaning back is counterintuitive and gives the false impression that you are retreating or cowering away; it also draws the attention up, all the while....

Leaning-back Stealth Groin Stop Kick

Another variation, mentioned previously, is the Hooking Groin Kick that is especially indicated if you kick the opponent's groin from behind. The kick is also working well from the front, but it then requires to go further between the opponent's legs before impact, what is not always practical. The 'hooking' effect is similar to the Essential 'hooking' Back Kicks presented in previous work. The principle is to hit the groin from down under, and then pull the kick back in while still going up, therefore hooking into the crotch and pulling it out. Easier to do than to explain.

Hook into the groin for more damage

The next example, illustrated at the top of next page, is an applied version of the 'Side Front Kick' version of the Groin Front Kick. The Side Front Kick, described in our book about Essential Kicks, is simply a Front Kick delivered sideways or obliquely to the outside. The kick development is fully 'front kick', but the angle of attack is oblique and surprising. In the Illustrations, a Low Kick is evaded forward and stopped/countered smoothly by a naturally-flowing Groin Kick.

Evade forward and out while punching; the rear foot goes directly to the groin

Groin Kicks are also techniques of choice when you are on the *ground*: you are difficult to strike and the shins and groin of your opponent are within easy range of your feet. If your opponent is not a grappler or a groundfighter, being on the ground can be a very advantageous position. Many examples are given in '**Ground Kicks**'. The example presented below is not typical, as it starts from a kneeling position, but it is interesting and a very good kicking drill in itself.

A traditional Jiu Jitsu series: Evasion and Catch, Ground Front Groin Kick, Stomp and Push

The last two examples will be a reminder of the importance of the Groin Kick in **Self Defense**. It is quite obvious that the opponent's groin should be a target of choice in a real confrontation. But here is the place to make two important points to remember. *First*, it should be noted that a real-life Groin Kick still needs to be **powerful** and to penetrate the target for a few inches. In spite of the sensitivity of the target, a weak touch will not be enough in an adrenaline- laden situation. Remember that you could also miss the precise target, and only the shock of a powerful approximation will be enough to rattle the opponent. Always kick as powerfully as possible, train for power and always kick into the target.

The *second* point to be made is that even a powerful groin kick on target can be found lacking; and I have seen it with my own eyes. High adrenaline, drugs, alcohol and mental illness can make people impervious to pain. Groin Kicks are intended to inflict searing pain in order to finish a fight. If the opponent does not feel pain, the kick is close to useless, together with most other techniques. In the case of a fight with an assailant on drugs or otherwise pain-free, there are only two alternatives: *limb destruction or choke.*

A *limb destruction*, like breaking some of his arms or leg joints, will make him unable to keep attacking you or run after you. The knee or ankle joints are targets of choice, but elbows, fingers, wrists and shoulder are valid; stomping or kicking the joints in the 'wrong' direction are possible techniques (to be described in our coming book about *Joint Kicks*). The other way to win a fight against such assailants is *choking* them to unconsciousness; it requires serious training, self-control and has a big disadvantage if there is more than one attacker (in that case you should back to a wall and use the opponent being choked as a temporary shield). Choking is a discipline that needs serious training under a qualified instructor.

This said, groin kicks are usually an excellent weapon in a real-life confrontation. In the first example below, you pre-empt or 'time-stop' an attack by a stick-wielding attacker. Get control of the armed hand while punching, kick the groin while his attention is on your grab, follow up with an elbow strike for example.

Offensive application of a groin kick in Self Defense

The last example will remind you to kick the groin as soon as it is possible. As an assailant attempts to take you in an underarm bear hug from behind, you *immediately* strike his head with a rear circular elbow (while bending forward to clear the target). Strike his clasped hands and get hold of a finger. Spin-back while pushing the finger back and down, and kick the groin as soon as in position. Follow up with another elbow strike, *while keeping hold of the finger*.

Rear Bear Hug release: kick the groin as soon as you get to face the opponent

4. THE HIGH-CHAMBERED STOMP FRONT KICK

Mae Fumikomi (Karatedo)

General

The stomp in a clinching situation

Stomp Kicks need full chambering to deserve the appellation 'stomp'. They are extremely easy to learn and very effective against a whole array of targets that we will mention here. Of course, it is, again, a kick of choice for self-defense, especially if you are wearing hard soled shoes. A well-executed Stomp Kick can achieve total limb destruction and neutralize an assailant; think crushed foot or sprained knee.

Stomp kicks, although more in their Side Kick-forms, do appear in traditional *Karate* forms, which give them definite "Lettres de Noblesse". It is therefore a must for the serious Martial Artist to practice and master them.

The Stomp is also obviously ideal for very close combat (See Photos)

The Stomp Kick in a classic **Krav Maga** application

Description

The Figure shows the delivery: you simply lift the knee forward in a full chambering, and then straighten the leg down directly towards the target in a crushing motion. Do *not* let your upper body extend up (as if straightening) while stomping: crouch with the stomp in order to put your whole body into the downward movement and in order *not* dissipate energy. According to the circumstances, you can either chamber (partly) back or let the foot land and stay on the target. You connect with the whole arch of the foot

or the heel only. According of the target you are hitting, you can also tilt the foot outwards, with no other difference of execution: You will have to do that if you aim for the ankle joint from the front as shown here, or for the back of the knee (as shown in the Photo above).

There is a variation of the kick which allows for even more power into the stomp: just like with the *Hikite* of Karate punches, you lift the standing foot **while stomping** with the other from the chamber position. The Illustration shows the execution on a focus pad.

Hop while stomping

Key points

- Chamber as *high* as possible for power.
- Keep you *guard* up, as you are in close range.
- Kick *through* the target, do not rebound on its surface. Think about crushing an insect...
- *Crouch* with the upper body while kicking and put your whole body into the movement

Targets

Everything you can stomp on, according to the relative situation to the opponent: toes, thigh, back of the knee, Achilles' heel, hands (especially fingers), head, ribs, armpit, ankle from all angles, front and side knee. All those attacks are illustrated by photos throughout the text of the section. And there are many more...

Typical Applications

The Photos below show an interesting application of the Stomp Kick, targeting the front *thigh* of an opponent: you chamber *high* as a feint, letting your opponent believe that you are trying to deliver a Penetrating Front Kick to the body or face. But you will stomp-kick his front thigh from your upper chambered position. This is a very surprising and painful kick.

The high chamber when targeting the thigh acts as a misdirecting feint

The Figures below show the most classic use of the Kick: the **Outward-tilted version** to the back of the knee. You evade, block, overstretch and redirect a fully committed Front Kick to find yourself on the blind out-side of the attacker; or you may even "have" his full back. You immediately grab both his shoulders and stomp-kick the back of his knee. Follow up with a hammer-fist strike to his face or to his clavicle, for example.

The applied classic Stomp to the back of the knee

Specific training

You **have** to train for *power*, for understanding the importance of the high *chambering* and for feeling the effect at *impact*, which can be surprising if you are not used to it. Crushing kicks do not come naturally and power training <u>must be drilled</u>. Practice both the classic version and the outward-tilted variation on a lying heavy bag, on a medicine ball, on a lying tire, on a focus pad,... Drill! Low Kicks require training!

Self defense

Most applications will be described here, in the Self defense section, as they are rather gruesome and more suitable to a self-defense situation or to a MMA contest, than the milder settings of regular classes or sport tournaments. But please read first and carefully the following words of caution:

<u>A stomp is an extremely effective and aggressive maneuver, as the "target" is held in place by the floor. When executing it in a self-defense situation, you should carefully consider the ethical and legal aspects: Are you justified in causing serious bodily harm to your aggressor in this situation? In fact you could rephrase this: Would a judge or a jury consider your action necessary to safeguard your own safety or that of others, or could you just have left the scene or taken less brutal action with no danger? And take into account that stomping a downed opponent will look to any witness as brutal and going against every ingrained fair-play sense of normative citizens.</u>

The following Photos show the use of the Stomp Kick against an opponent brought to his knees (in quadruped position), but the principles stay true if the opponent lies on the floor in any position. If you are behind him or to his side: Stomp his Achilles' tendon. If you are in front of him: Stomp on his hand or fingers. Remember the legal and ethical ramifications: Stomp on his Achilles' heel only if he keeps attacking after being taken down, and in order to make sure he cannot pursue you, but nothing more. Stomping on his fingers could be justified for example, if he is armed or if he keeps grabbing you from the floor to prevent your escaping.

Stomp onto Achilles' tendon only if warranted

Stomp onto wrist or fingers in Self-Defense situations

Next Photos show the use of the Kick against an opponent you have just downed or thrown and who is lying on his back in front of you. He will probably lift his legs

between you in something of a ground guard. As soon as he does that, grab his ankles and throw them forcefully aside to make him roll slightly on his side; *immediately* stomp his ribs or head.

Stomp the ribs of a downed opponent

If warranted, you can stomp the head of a downed opponent as he lies on the back or on his side

If you have good control of the downed opponent's legs and hold both his feet, you can stomp him while going *between* his legs: in his groin (Self-explanatory, not illustrated),

in his body (See Photos), or in his face (See Photos). It is **imperative** that you move away after the kick, *as illustrated*: You are in a rather dangerous position, especially against an experienced grappler.

Stomp the plexus or ribs while keeping control of the legs

Do not stay between his legs after the stomp: This is a dynamic attack

The Figures below show a classic use of the Stomp Kick for self-defense, as a follow-up to a take-down which keeps control of the opponent's arm (This is applicable to nearly all Judo or Jiu-Jitsu throws!). In this example, the assailant grabs your lapel. Before he can hit you, you grab his hand and step behind his front leg while striking his biceps with your forearm. You then pivot to throw him to the ground by reaping his leg but you keep hold of his grabbing arm. As soon as he hits the ground, you **stomp into his armpit** while pulling on the arm. You could then pivot and get down on your knee to break his elbow on your thigh. This is a very dangerous technique.

Stomping the offered armpit is a crippling technique

The next Photos show the stomp as the natural follow-up to a high knee strike. The knee strike takes the additional function of the high chamber! From a clinch position in which you hold your opponent's head with both hands, you side-step to your opponent's side while releasing with your further hand. You now push his head down with both hands while kneeing his face from your side position. *From the high kneeing position* you stomp his foot forcefully. Follow up. This is a very surprising and useful combination from the clinch, as your opponent does not expect the (simultaneous) hand-release and side-step.

Evade, knee and stomp

And the next Photos show an interesting and slightly exotic variation of the classical Stomp Kick: stomping down on the back of his knee from your position in front of him (basically in a clinch where you overtake his leg from the outside). It would be recommended to attack his face simultaneously with an arm strike.

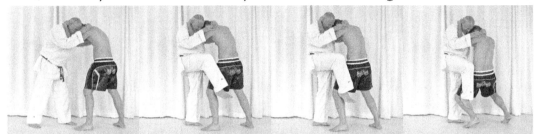
Surprise: Attack his back knee from the front

The coming Illustrations show an *offensive* combination starting with a double-leg takedown ("Shoot"): As soon as you lift his legs while pushing back and he starts falling down, you stand up and *stomp*-kick him between the legs. Having so "softened" him, you can now set up an ankle-lock and then *stomp* him again on the knee of the lying leg. You then can keep the stomping foot in place for pain and better control of the ankle-lock.

Shoot, stomp the groin, lock the leg, stomp the knee

The next Illustrations show the use of the painful **Scraping** Stomp Kick in a clinching situation. *Scraping* has been mentioned in the section about the Soccer Low Front Kick. This example below shows the full scraping version of the Kick, with the stomping foot staying on top of the opponent's foot, as a foot trap, *while you push him down*.

You kick directly into grating position (with a straight Front Kick) and then stomp by gliding along the shin!

Soccer low Front Kick to the knee, then **scraping** *Stomp to the ankle*

The next Photos show the classic counter to a "come-along" arm-lock, in which you stomp the back of the opponent's knee without having to tilt your foot, because of your relative position to the attacker. You can follow-up with a dangerous Achilles' tendon stomp if the situation warrants it.

Classic release from standing "come-along" Figure-4 arm-lock

We have already seen a stomp on the knee to facilitate a leg-lock. The next Figures describe a similar application: Stomp the knee joint and **use the stomp** to stay in control of the opponent. In this example, you evade a Side Kick by retreating your hips *just enough*, and get control of his foot with an "X- block" from above (Remember *Shorinji Kempo's Hiki-Mi* mentioned in the Introduction). Twist his foot for a full turn-and-a-half, in order to take him down in a full somersault. Keep control of his foot while you stomp on the knee of his other leg. Keep your foot on the knee while you twist his foot in a painful ankle-lock.

Stomp the knee and keep it in place for better control

You remember the stomp to the armpit after a throw. The drawings show the classical use of the Stomp Kick *to the ribs* as another immediate follow-up to a successful throw. As your assailant catches your wrist, you pivot to his outside, circle his wrist from the outside to reverse the grip, and hit him with a palm strike to the side of the face. Having taken control of his attacking arm, you pull him forward while encircling his neck from behind and putting him in arm-lock position. Hit the neck with the arm forcefully as you

get into position. As he starts to resist the move, you reverse the momentum, pulling his head back by the chin to throw him back over your thigh. As he falls to the floor you stomp his ribs in an uninterrupted flow of the maneuver.

The natural Stomp to the ribs after a take-down

 3

 4

 5

 6

The next Figures show the use of the kick to painfully *draw the opponent's attention away* from an evading move that you are starting. In this case, as the assailant grips your hair from the front, you immediately catch his wrist to reduce pain (and to control him), *while* delivering a Stomp Kick to his front foot. Use the pain created for a classic release: disentangle yourself by retreating and pivoting to place his arm in arm-lock position. Follow up.

Nothing like a stomp to soften an opponent for more incoming techniques

The Illustrations below show another natural use of the kick, as an integral part of a *rear choke* technique (*Hadaka Jime – Judo*). You evade and control from the outside a downward stick strike; and you then catch his lapel as high as possible with your rear hand. Moving to his back, you use your other elbow to push the back of his neck while pulling on his lapel. In this classic choke position, stomp the back of his knee.

The rear-knee Stomp is a natural for choking maneuvers from behind

We have already seen the Stomp as a natural continuation of a high knee strike, the knee strike taking the role of the high chamber. We will share another example of a rear-knee Stomp from behind the opponent; but, this time, the knee strike will be an **arm-break** and there will be no landing of the foot in-between. As shown in the Figures below, you evade a downward knife attack by stepping forward and to his out-side while controlling his descending arm. Stay very close to his back while getting control of the knife wrist. Try to catch his throat from behind with your other hand, while delivering a full-powered circular knee strike to his kidneys. Keep hold of the throat, (or chin or shoulder) while trying to break his (knife) elbow joint with an upward knee strike of the other leg (Turn the wrist to position the elbow down!). *From the high knee position*, stomp directly down into the back of his knee.

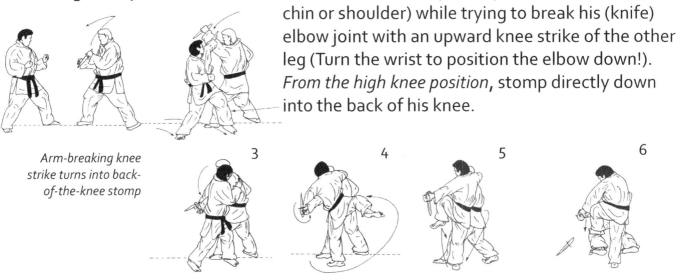

Arm-breaking knee strike turns into back-of-the-knee stomp

The next Drawings illustrate an interesting last use of the stomp kick: *to keep your opponent's foot in place until you can come and catch it for further use!* The example also shows a fast **front-leg** Stomp Kick. In this instance, an aggressor gets hold of your wrist from your side. Before he can complete his attack, stomp fast from the *front leg* onto his front foot. Immediately bend forward and extend your arm down and towards him to dissolve the hold. In a smooth follow-up, deliver a flowing upward elbow strike below his chin. Keep your Stomp on his foot *to keep it in place*, until you can bend and catch it with your other hand coming in between your legs. Lift his ankle while pushing his upper body back to throw him to the ground, where you'll *stomp* (again) his groin.

Fast front-leg Stomp Kick with the purpose of keeping his foot in place

Addendum

We shall start these few illustrative additions with the attacking of an opponent from **behind** (in a possible situation where your loved ones or especially helpless victims are threatened). The Stomp Front Kick can then target the assailant's Achille's tendon to neutralize him. This is a dangerous, potentially crippling, technique. Caution is warranted.

Stomp Achille's tendon from behind: dangerous

Then comes an additional application of the (already mentioned) Front Stomp Kick to the **thigh**: block and redirect a Front Kick to stomp the sensitive *side thigh* of the landing leg.

Stomp the thigh of the opponent's landing leg

Referring to the section about stomping a **downed** opponent, it should be added that: if you still have control of one of his arms, you should then *pull on it while stomping* for much more effect.

*The **Pull-in** Front Stomp Kick*

Last but not least, we shall present another application of the **back-of-the-knee Stomp executed from the front**. This example will go all the way to ground control. The technique can be applied offensively or as part of a side-forward evasion against a punching attack. In any case, as soon as you have the standing side choke, *stomp his back knee* to bring him down. Keep a tight carotid choke all the time while bringing him down. Chokes are very dangerous techniques to be used only in relevant situations and to be practiced carefully.

In Side Choke, use the Stomp Kick to take him down for ground control

5. THE TILTED-HEEL LOW FRONT KICK

General

This very important kick is simply the low version of the *Essential* Tilted-heel Front Kick already mentioned. It is a *Penetrating Kick* in this case, -**not** a Stomp Kick-, and it should be practiced as such. Because it is penetrating and directed down, it has some feeling of stomping that is important to take into account. But on the whole, it is a *snap* kick that requires chambering back after impact a few inches **into** the target, just like the basic Essential version.

The kick is very typical of East-Asian styles, like Indonesian *Pencak Silat*, and of the soft styles of *Kung Fu* (I have even seen it named the "Hsing-I Kick" by *Hsing-I* practitioners). It is also in use in many other styles though, and it should be mentioned that it is a great universal Stop Kick (See first Photo).

The target, -usually the knee from all sides-, is struck with the arch of the foot or (preferably) with the heel.

The Tilted-heel Front Kick
as a stop-kick

The Tilted-heel Front Kick
to the knee

The Tilted-heel Front Kick
to the back of the knee

The Tilted-heel Front Kick
to the side of the knee

Description

The Figure describes the orthodox delivery of the kick: chamber just like for a regular Penetrating Front Kick, and then extend the leg straight into the target while tilting the foot outwards. Connect with the heel part of the arch of the foot, and thrust the

hips forward into the kick, just like for any other penetrating kick. If the circumstances dictate, you can slightly lean backwards while thrusting the hips forward. **Recoil** forcefully.

Key points

- Keep your *guard up*.
- This is not a stomp: *chamber back* after kicking an inch into the target.
- Use the *hips* for the thrusting movement.

Targets

The knee, from all sides. Also the front thigh and the upper shin.

Typical Applications

The Illustrations show a typical application of the kick: Attacking a landing kicking leg. In this case, you block and redirect a Hopping Side Kick from your opponent, forcing him to land forward a bit off-balance. You keep control of his front hand, and immediately use your rear leg for a Tilted-heel Low Front Kick to the side of his knee. Follow up with one of my favorite combinations: use the same leg, -without landing the foot-, to throw a Roundhouse Kick to his face, as he pivots and bends down on account of the hit knee.

Try to always low-kick a landing leg

In a variation of the previous application, you can also low-kick the landing leg with your front foot and then follow with a high Roundhouse Kick from the other (rear) leg, as shown in the Photos.

The front-leg Tilted-heel Low Front Kick to a landing knee

The following Figures show again the *front-leg* variation in its preferred application as a **stop-kick**. The classic way to drill this application is in the "cat stance" common to all traditional arts from Japan, Okinawa, China or Indonesia. In this stance, called *Neko Ashi Dachi* in Japanese, the front leg is weightless; <u>although it is advised to make that fact as unnoticeable as possible</u>. As soon as your opponent shows signs of launching any attack, you lift the front knee; you can simultaneously extend your hand towards his eyes as a distraction. You kick his front knee as he starts moving.

Front-leg stop-kick from the Cat Stance

The next Drawings show the classic targeting of the sensitive **back-of-the-knee**. It is presented at the end of an application starting with a variation of the rearwards evasion, that this time also includes a pulling back of the front leg. As your opponent attacks you with a Spin-back Back Kick, you retreat just enough to evade the kick while controlling it. You pull the hips and the leg back *just enough*, but keep a forward upper body for better blocking and faster countering. Your airborne leg does roundhouse-kick his landing leg; and you land it deep forwards on his out-side while blocking an eventual natural back-fist strike follow-up. You are very much in his back now, and take control of his arm and shoulder while using your rear leg for the Low Front Kick into the back of his knee. Follow up.

To use whenever possible: the Tilted-heel Front Low Kick to the back of the knee

The last Figures show a special application of the kick, interesting although probably too sophisticated for casual use. You block an incoming Front Kick with an outside knee sweep of the front leg. From this **high knee position**, you attack *directly* his standing knee in a Tilted-heel Low Front Kick. You can follow up with a ridge-hand strike to the side of his head as he stumbles. It is a great drill for speed and flexibility, and it can be used by experienced artists in appropriate situations.

Special but surprising: the chamber of the kick is a knee block

Specific training

This is a kick that needs drilling in order to differentiate him clearly from a stomp. Practice on a **tire and a lying bag,** while concentrating on the *recoil.*

Self defense

The following Photos show a very punishing combination that can be used *after any successful use of the ubiquitous Straight-leg Low Roundhouse Kick* (Generic "Low kick"). In this example, you evade, block and redirect your assailant's kick, so that you find yourself on his *out-side*, and can deliver a punishing Straight-leg Roundhouse to the thigh of his landing leg. You then grab both his shoulders and deliver a full-hipped Tilted-heel Front Kick to the back of his knee. While you recoil and lower the foot, get hold of his head by the chin and/or hair, and pivot while pulling his head back. Pull the head back and down while hitting it with a powerful upward knee strike. Lower the knee while pulling him down. Careful with this dangerous combination!

In this punishing combination the Tilted-heel Front Kick is used to place the assailant off-balance to his rear

The coming Figures illustrate a combination drilled into me in *Wado-ryu Karate* practice a long time ago. The *Wado-ryu* style of Karate is still close to its *Ju-Jitsu* roots and relies a lot onto evading techniques and body movement (*Tai Sabaki*). In this example, you provoke your assailant into a committed Reverse Punch counter by **feinting a side move** to your in-side while leaning slightly forward. As your opponent punches in the direction you are going, you switch directions and evade circularly to your out-side while jabbing (*Nagashi Tsuki, typical of Wado-ryu*). You immediately catch his extending arm while front-kicking his front knee from the side. There is a Kung Fu version of this maneuver that is illustrated by following set of Photos.

The Tilted-heel Front Kick to the side of the knee in an evading exercise typical **of Wado-ryu Karate**

Evade the reverse punch while kicking the inside knee

And finally, the next Photos show in turn a typical *Wing Chung*-inspired combination, blocking three punches, catching the attacking arm and kicking punishingly, again, the side of the front knee.

Block, block, block, catch, kick

6. THE LOW ROUNDHOUSE KICK

Gedan Mawashi Geri (Karatedo), Te Ka/Te Tad Lang (Muay Thai)

General

This, again, is a very simple but versatile kick: It a classic *Essential* Roundhouse Kick, but delivered below the belt. Please refer to previous work for the background about Roundhouse Kicks. The kick is of course different from the Straight-leg Roundhouse Low Kick presented later in the next section (7). Because of the low targets, the kick is more of a *regular* Roundhouse-type or even of a *small* Roundhouse-type, rather than a full Roundhouse (Refer to *Essential Kicks'* theory). The amount of chambering is, of course up to you, but some chambering is needed, as this a **whipping** kick that needs to be recoiled.

This is a very fast kick, which can also be delivered from the front leg, and therefore is a great tool to *harass* the opponent or to start an offensive combination. The side Photos show a classic *cross-step delivery of the front-leg version* of the kick, targeting the inner knee of the opponent's front leg.

Attrition-kick or leg-opener

An ubiquitous and versatile kick

Description

The Figure shows the classic delivery connecting with the ball of the foot: chamber the knee (but not above the height of the target) with the leg at about 45 degrees; *not* a Full Roundhouse chamber, but *not* a Small Roundhouse front chamber either. Deliver a snappy kick with fast recoil. Connect with the ball of the foot (as illustrated) or the top of the foot. Of course all variations are valid: chamber from full to small, height of knee, relative straightening of the leg...

The Low Roundhouse Kick

Key points

- This is a speed kick: *avoid telegraphing* moves, upper body as immobile as possible.
- Keep you *guard up*.
- *Recoil* fast and forcefully after penetrating slightly into the target.

Targets

The groin, all sides of the thigh (See Photos), the knee, the shins and calves. Also the ankles as shown. Of course, everything else if the opponent is down or kneeling.

Low Roundhouse Toe Kick to the inside thigh   *Low Roundhouse Kick to the outside ankle*   *Low Roundhouse Kick to the inside ankle*

Typical Applications

The Illustrations show a very simple but effective variation applied to a Self-Defense situation. As the **groin** is the target, there is no need for any chambering: the *front* foot just lifts and travels *directly* towards the target. The distance is covered by hopping <u>after the front leg has started moving</u>, just as in the *Essential* Front-leg Hopping Roundhouse. You can follow up with a second Low Roundhouse or Straight-leg Low Roundhouse Kick, from the other leg.

Lift the leg directly towards the assailant's groin while hopping forward

The next Illustrations, at the top of next page, show the already-mentioned targeting of the ankle, from both a rear-leg and a front-leg attack, after feinting high. This is not a sweep but a painful kick, with the usual added effect of putting the opponent somewhat off-balance. Kick with ball of the foot or the lower tibia (shinbone). Of course, always follow up. This kick, delivered with the lower shin to the side or back of the ankle, is called "Nias" by south-American *Shoot* practitioners. ➤

*Low rear-leg Roundhouse to **outside** ankle*

*Low front-leg Roundhouse to the **inside** ankle*

We have already seen the kick aiming for the inside thigh, and connecting with the ball of the foot. The Figures below show the use of the fast *front-leg* variation in a very effective **hi/lo/hi/lo** combination: Jab and deliver the kick (Front-leg Roundhouse to the inside thigh). Just lift the leg directly into the kick, fast and loose. Lower the leg into a Cross Punch, which will in turn pull your hip and a Straight-leg Roundhouse to the outside of the same thigh.

The variation without the Cross (=Reverse Punch) is illustrated by the following Photos series: *High* jab, *low* inside toe kick, *low* outside toe kick.

The front-leg Low Roundhouse is a natural follow-up of the jab

Hi/Lo inside/Lo outside

As mentioned, this kick is fast and a great combination starter. The Photos *at the top of next page* show a classic combination starting with a fast hopping version of the kick to close the distance to your opponent (The front-leg fast hopping version is clearly illustrated above by illustrations on the previous page). From opposite stances in the example, you chamber the front leg while pushing forward into a hop, and then kick your opponent's outer thigh. Your body slightly leans back. As the opponent's attention is down, you land with a high jab/cross combination, followed by a full-powered rear-leg Full Roundhouse Kick to the head. The rationale behind this application is close to that of Feint Kicks of the **leg tap-type**, which purpose is just to draw attention down as you punch up.

➡

Low Roundhouse Kick as a fast and low misdirection before a classic jab/cross/high Roundhouse

Specific training

This kick needs to be drilled for **speed,** not power. Train both the rear-leg and the front-leg versions on the hanging heavy bag.

Self defense

The Photos below show the use of the kick against a downed opponent. Ideally, you should catch his hand as a diversion and to prevent blocking, and release it during the delivery of the kick. Remember to chamber back!

Kick a falling or standing-up opponent, if warranted

Aim at catching his hand while kicking

Same maneuver with the other leg

I have underlined the importance of the chamber-back for this kick. But rules often need exceptions. The Drawings show an interesting special variation of the kick which is used to "catch" and lift your opponent's leg. You deliver the Low Roundhouse from your front leg to your assailant's inside knee, but you do not chamber back; instead, you "hook" with your ankle behind his knee, *while kicking through **and** lifting*. You catch his lifted leg with your rear hand, while keeping him away and under control with your lead hand. You lower your kicking leg and you can then kick his standing leg or just push him to the floor. This is a great drill to learn kick sensitivity, and it should be practiced regularly by experienced artists.

The Low Roundhouse as a leg-pick-up opener

One of the specific self-defense uses of this kick is described in the coming Photos. Use the kick to *open* the assailant's legs and *set his groin up for a follow-up kick.* In this example, you deliver a rear-leg kick to the inside thigh, recoil, and without lowering the kicking foot, you deliver a fast upward Groin Kick (as described in section 3) from the chambered-back position. If you have difficulties in executing the double kick, you can also lower the kicking foot and let it rebound on the ground for the second kick. This is all about speed; so drill for it. This is also a very important exercise for general kicking proficiency.

A fast and devastating little double kick

We have mentioned the attrition aspect of the kick and we have shown the use of the kick to the inside-front leg to "open" the opponent. The attack to the inner front leg is very disturbing and it is therefore a great distance closer at the beginning of an offensive combination. The coming Photos show its use to prepare for a MMA "shoot", - a two-legs tackle.

A fast Low Roundhouse to the inside knee will rattle your opponent to allow for your follow-up

If one inside-knee Roundhouse works, two should work even better! The following Photos show the use of *two* Roundhouse Kicks to the *inside* legs to prepare for a knee strike.

Kick one inside knee, then the other; catch your wobbly opponent's neck for a knee strike

And the next Photos show a great application of the Low Roundhouse into the *inside front knee*, in which you commit yourself to a powerful attack and kick **through** the opponent's knee. This time, this is *not* a prodding or an attrition kick; this is a **crippling** attack. Your momentum takes you then into a natural spin-back that you conclude with an Essential Short Back Kick (This is how the kick is delivered in Muay Thai: kick-through).

Kick through and let your momentum take you into a spin-back

The coming Figures, at the top of next page, show the use of the kick in a situation in which you have caught an assailant's kick and hold him standing on one leg. In the example, you block his Roundhouse Kick and encircle his leg to hold it firmly from below; simultaneously reverse-punch him in the face. You can then hook-punch the inside thigh you are holding up. Start then to roundhouse-kick the knee of the leg he is standing on with your front-leg (= the side you are using to hold him). You can throw him down when you decide, either by sweeping his standing leg, lifting his caught-up leg, or with the illustrated joint-damaging knee-over-shoulder takedown (Be extremely careful in practice!). ➤

A great kick to attrite his knee after you have caught one of his legs

The next Drawings make, to conclude, a very important self-defense point. You have downed your attacker to the ground with a punch, a kick or a take-down. As he starts getting up, you see his hand going for his belt or his pocket, probably reaching for a weapon: a knife, a stick, a gun, a pepper spray or a taser. Do not hesitate, ever. In this case, deliver a Roundhouse Kick to the side of his neck at full power; front-leg or rear-leg as most natural to you. Take no chances, and follow up by stomping his fingers for example, to make him unable to efficiently use a weapon in the near future.

In case you suspect he could be armed, do not hesitate to kick a downed assailant

Illustrative Photos

The Essential Full Roundhouse Kick

*The Essential **Small** Roundhouse Kick*

The Essential Front-leg Hopping Roundhouse Kick

Addendum

As a Stop Kick, the Low Roundhouse Kick is best used as a 'timing' kick and aiming at the groin. In the example extracted from '**Stop Kicks**', you catch an opponent in the middle of a his hop for a front-leg kick attack. Simple and gruesomely effective. Follow up with a Straight-leg kick-through Roundhouse to the knee or thigh.

Low Roundhouse 'timing' Stop Kick

In our book about '**Stealth Kicks**', we underline the importance of Low Kicks as attacks difficult to spot early. But the application of the Low Roundhouse that we shall present will be different: it will be the use as a misdirecting *Tap Kick* (already mentioned). You use the fast front-leg Low Roundhouse to the opponent's front lower leg as a *distraction* that will allow scoring with a *high* Backfist strike. Follow up with a full-powered rear-leg kick-through Crescent Kick, for example.

Low Roundhouse Tap Kick will open the opponent to high strikes

We will conclude with an unecessary reminder of the importance of groin-kicking in real life situations. In self defense, kick towards your assaillant's groin as soon as possible. It will sometimes be a Front Kick, it will sometimes be a Roundhouse Kick, it will be sometimes another kick type. In the example, you duck a stick attack and immediately strike the opponent's open groin with a fast **Roundhouse**. Control his striking hand which has passed you over, and follow up with a hip-powered punch *while you pull on his arm*.

Evade and kick the groin first

7. THE LOW STRAIGHT-LEG ROUNDHOUSE KICK

Low kick (Common name), Martelo Baixo (Capoeira), Te Tut (Muay Thai)

General

This is without any doubt the low kick par excellence, and it is the way it used to be commonly referred to at the start of the Full-Contact craze of the late Seventies: The **Low Kick**. This kick is the bread and butter of the full-contact fighting sports, because of its efficacy and the many opportunities in which it can be used. This kick is typical of the hardest of Martial Arts, like *Kyokushinkai Karate* and *Muay Thai* boxing; it is frequently used in MMA and Kickboxing tournaments.

The kick is in fact a basic *Essential* kick described in detail in previous work, but a book about *Low Kicks* would certainly be incomplete without it; and so we shall still describe it here again. We still recommend though that you consult our previous treatise about *Essential Kicks* for more theory and additional applications.

One of the best kicks for Self-defense

Various examples of applied "Low Kicks"

Description

The Figures, at the top of next page, describe the execution of the kick: You first pivot with the shoulders and the hips, and then only launch the quasi-straight leg directly into the target. In the *Muay Thai* version of the kick, you keep the pivoting momentum and kick *through* the target to such an extent that, should you miss the target, you would complete a nearly full turn (See Photos further on). In the more controlled version, you would start pivoting back with the shoulders and hips as the leg is released forward.

...It is generally a rear-leg kick, but, when delivered below the belt, even the front-leg version is powerful enough to inflict serious damage.

You connect with the top of the foot, the front of the ankle or,-preferably-, the *shin*. This kick is very important and should be practiced in all possible footwork variations, some of which will be presented here. Note that the kick can also be delivered while leaning back with the upper body, which sometimes is justified by safety reasons.

The hips pull the kick in

Trade off of the power version: If you miss a kick-through, the momentum can carry you far out

Comparative top view of the straight-leg- and the regular- Roundhouse Kick

Key points

- The power of the kick comes from the *hip*: The leg is just an extension. Concentrate on kicking with the whole body.
- Keep your *guard up.*
- Always kick *through* the target, for a few inches at least.

Targets

For the purpose of this "Low Kicks" book: Hip, thigh, knee, shin and calf, ankle. But, generally speaking, the kick can be used to target very successfully the ribs, the kidneys, the upper back, the neck and the head.

The usual and most natural target is the outside thigh (the outside knee in self-defense), and many examples will be given.

But the front of the thigh is also a valuable target, although it needs some footwork to be put in range, as shown in the Photos.

Jab while evading outside and deliver the Roundhouse Kick to the front of the opponent's thigh

...Another example of a very natural combination leading to positioning for a "Low Kick" to the *front of the thigh* is presented in turn in the next Photos set: A first regular Low kick/reverse punch combination (lowering the foot to the *outside*) is followed by

a jab or lead-hand hook while *pivoting away from the centerline*. (This is a typical *Wadoryu Karatedo* punch called **Nagashi Tsuki**). You are now in perfect position (perpendicular) for a full-powered straight-leg roundhouse to the front of his thigh.

The combination will place you in perfect position for a front-of-the-thigh kick

Typical Applications

The Drawings show a '**front-leg by forward cross-step**'- application of the kick,

targeting the *inner thigh*. In this example, you jab while cross-stepping (or even while hopping). The purpose of the Jab is to limit his field of vision. Follow up. Simple but effective!

Jab while stepping to keep his attention high

As we mentioned, the kick should be practiced with all possible footwork variations. The next Photos show a very important variation of the previous cross-step, which is basically a **low-flying** "Low kick"! You lunge with the front leg and kick with the rear leg, but as the switch will happen *in mid-air*, it is definitely a Jumping Kick (The rear leg starts to lift *before* the front leg lands in position). I recommend drilling this version a lot; trying to gradually increase the distance you cover with the jump. Even if you will not use this kick ever, the drill is great for positioning skills and for general kicking proficiency.

The "flying" Straight-leg Low Roundhouse Kick

...The next Figures present a classic, very simple and very effective combination opening, based on the *Progressive Indirect Attack* (PIA) principle, very much touted by *Jeet Kune Do* stylists. You start with an exaggerated jab towards the opponent's groin, which trajectory will change as soon as he reacts, and will then evolve into a high jab towards his *eyes*. This convoluted hand movement is in fact a cover for the coming rear-leg Straight-leg Roundhouse to the outer thigh. Follow up.

Simple and effective combination based on the PIA principle

And the next Drawings show the kick delivered from an **angled** position, resulting in targeting the hip joint or, again, the front of the thigh. This is a very effective kick, and moreover, it also flows very naturally into a full-hipped Hook Punch follow-up. As your opponent initiates a high Reverse Punch (*Cross*), you slip to the *outside* of his arm while controlling it (or blocking it) and you deliver the rear-leg kick into his hip joint (**Lo**). Lower the leg back rearwards in order to gather momentum for a full-powered Hook Punch to the head (**Hi**).

Attack the opponent's front by evading into position

The Figures at the top of next page show another **angled** delivery, this time to the *back* of the leg and from the out-side. This variation is presented in order to illustrate the importance of this 'Low Kick' in nearly all possible situations, and from all angles. As your opponent lifts his arm and by doing so telegraphs his intention to wide-punch, you slide in to catch his neck with your lead hand, while protecting your head with your shoulder. Your opponent's punch should fly over your ducking and tucked head. You then pull his head into an uppercut, and step *forward and to the side* while keeping the pull on his head. You keep pivoting while pushing him down and away. From this full side position, and in his blind spot, you launch your "Low Kick" to the back of his thigh (or knee).

➡

Position yourself for the Low Kick to the back of his legs

And the coming Figures will present the classic use of the Low kick on to the **landing** kicking leg of an opponent, and then will show a very important possible follow-up, based on keeping your opponent off-balance after your kick has connected. The Straight-leg Low Roundhouse Kick is a very powerful maneuver, but it still often needs to be followed up to completion. In the example, you evade, block and redirect your opponent's rear-leg Penetrating Front Kick in order to find yourself on his *out-side*. As he lands, you deliver a full-hipped Straight-leg Roundhouse to the back of his thigh and you grab his shoulder. You lower your kicking leg and pivot on it for half-a-circle, while violently pulling him down and around and while keeping him off-balance. You then deliver a Roundhouse Kick with the other leg, to his head which should be 'coming' your way. If you are flexible enough, this can also be a more devastating Straight-leg **high** Roundhouse, - Muay Thai style-, something of a "high Low-Kick".

After a successful Low Kick, grab your opponent and pull him off-balance for more kicking

Specific training

The Straight-leg Roundhouse Kick should be drilled all the time and in all possible ways: hanging bag, standing bag, tire, protected sparring, and more. It should be drilled for speed and for power.
When drilling, always keep in mind the kicking **through** the target. Do *not slap* the target and do not slow the momentum when getting close to the target.
Power is important for this kick and general power training is important to its success: *PLYO-FLEX* Training is highly recommended for explosive power development.

Self defense

The Low Kick is of course a great kick for self-defense when properly executed: It is especially devastating against an untrained opponent who is not used to being hit powerfully in the lower limbs.

The coming Drawings show the use of the kick against the Low Kick itself. As your assailant attempts to kick your front leg, pull the target leg back, just enough, while keeping your body weight on your rear leg. Let your leg rebound and launch your own Straight-leg Roundhouse Kick to the *outside of his landing leg,* while grabbing his upper arm or shoulder. Pull him forward as you land behind him, and use your other leg to deliver a *second* Straight-leg Roundhouse to the calf of his other leg. This has the added effect of sweeping his front leg and make him fall down (Remember that it is not a

sweep but a real **kick**).You can meet his falling head with an Essential Hook Kick (as Illustrated) or with an Outside Crescent Kick from the same kicking leg. You could still follow up with another Roundhouse, to the head for example.

Low Kick vs. Low Kick. Then low-kick!

 3

 4 5

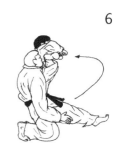 6

A variation on this theme is presented in the next Figures: a Low Kick to the front shin/ankle of the rear leg will be extremely painful and will cause a *frontal* fall! We shall present it in a tactically interesting application against an aggressive kicker. In a same-as-your-opponent stance, you feint with the upper body to "invite" the rear-leg Penetrating Front Kick of your opponent. But as soon as he starts his move you evade aggressively to the left in a full 90 degrees *Tai Sabaki.* As he lands, deliver the low Roundhouse to his ankle (It is a **Kick**, not a sweep!) and follow up as he lands on his face.

Position yourself for the Low Kick to the shin of the rear leg: painful takedown

The example presented in the next Figures is in the same vein and is, again, *not* to be confused with a sweep. The *Low Roundhouse Sweep* is presented in Chapter 8, coming next. Here we have a **kick** resulting in a very nasty fall, but still a kick and *not* a sweep. We will present it in a self-defense application against a knee-in-the-lower-back rear choke. But note that this kick variation is valid for any situation in which you catch your opponent's leg *from the inside*. When attacked with said rear choke and knee-in-back, you **immediately** take hold of the choking arm to relieve pressure, while pivoting strongly with a low block (*Gedan Barai – Karatedo*) to the knee in your back that turns into a scooping catch. The "block" is to be considered as an **attack** onto your opponent's limb, as always in *Shotokan Karate*: It is a painful strike to the side of the knee. You complete your pivot while lifting your assailant's knee and you find yourself in position for a full-powered Straight Leg Roundhouse *Kick* to the front of the knee of his *standing* leg. On top of the damage to his knee, this will result in a difficult-to-control and hard fall on his face. Follow up as he falls, by stomping his ankle for example.

Low Kick to the front of a standing leg hurts and causes a nasty fall

The Photos show a great application against the same downed opponent from the previous application: You get hold of one of his ankles and low-kick his outside thigh. This is an **Attrition Kick**: keep kicking, always going back out after each kick to assess the situation.

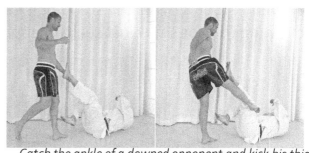

Catch the ankle of a downed opponent and kick his thigh repeatedly

The Drawings *at the top on next page* show another example of application against a Low Kick *attack*: If you do not have time to evade and pull your leg back, you must lift your leg to intercept the kick on the fleshy side of your shin, in order to minimize the damage, in a classic **Leg-Block**. Lower then the leg while punching him to the face (or the body, as per his guard), and immediately launch a rear-leg Low Kick to his ***inside thigh***; if possible while grabbing his front upper arm. Follow up, for example with *another* Low Kick from your other leg, to the out-side of his front leg this time. Follow up with more.

➡️

Two Low Kicks as a response to a leg-blocked Low Kick

Note that a natural follow-up of a successful powerful Straight-leg Roundhouse into the *outer thigh* of your opponent would be a classic **Scoop Throw** (*Sukui Nage – Judo*). The set-up is shown in the coming Photos. The throw is illustrated in the Illustrative Photos section.

The "Low Kick" is ideally followed up by Judo's **Sukui Nage**

And last but not least, let us remind the reader that the Straight-leg Roundhouse is in fact a variation of the *Roundhouse Kick*. Just like the *regular* Low Roundhouse Kick, the Straight-leg version is effective, and even more so, as a **"Cutting" Kick**. It will deliver an even harder blow to the standing knee or standing leg of your kicking assailant. The following Photos show just such an application.

Block and catch the kick; low-kick the standing leg with everything you have

Illustrative Photos and Illustrations

The Straight-leg Roundhouse Kick is an *Essential* basic Kick; it is generally a Low Kick, **but it can be delivered at high or mid-level** as well.

*The **high** Straight-leg Roundhouse in training...*

...and in tournament (Marc De Bremaeker)

The classic Essential Straight-leg Roundhouse to the inside knee (Ziv Faige)

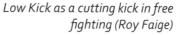

Low Kick as a cutting kick in free fighting (Roy Faige)

Remember that the upper body and the hips pull the kick in for extra power

Sukui Nage - *the natural takedown technique after a classic 'Low Kick'*

Addendum

And we shall conclude with an application extracted from '**Stealth Kicks**'. Feinting in one way or another will always give you the advantage of surprise; it is a sophisticated way to fight. The example below is what we called in 'Stealth Kicks': the Low Kick Feint to Stepping Low Kick. The technique is related to the Double Low Kick with airborne switching that we have already encountered in the Chapter. It is a pretty easy <u>misdirecting</u> maneuver to master and it is very effective. Deliver a fast front-leg Hopping 'Low Kick' to the inside knee of your opponent. It hurts and warrants attention. Repeat, but this time it will be a feint: switch legs airborne to deliver a powerful 'Low Kick' of the rear leg to the outside knee or even the lower ribs (illustrated) of the opponent.

Conditioning 'Low Kick' followed by Low Kick Feint turning into a Hopping Low Kick from the other leg

8. THE LOW STRAIGHT-LEG ROUNDHOUSE SWEEP

Banda (Capoeira), Gedan Mawashi Barai (Karatedo)

General

This is a *variation* of the Straight-leg Roundhouse Kick that we wanted to present separately, as the delivery is slightly different in its emphasis. This is a kick which purpose is to cause the opponent to fall down, but it is a painful **kick** first and a sweep only second. The felling of an opponent is of great psychological importance in a fight: Even if the technique is not a decision-maker, the fact that at the end of your kick the opponent lands on the floor will certainly hurt his self-confidence for the rest of the engagement. It is also spectacular and therefore disturbing to the other side. This kick is very much in use in *Kyokushinkai Karate* fighting, and in many other arts in some form or the other. The preferred use of the kick will always be as a **"Cutting" Kick**, i.e. kicking the standing leg of a kicking opponent, but, with good training, it is easy to perform on an adversary standing on both legs. It is a technique well worth drilling. It was a favorite technique of mine at the start of my career when sweeps were all the rage, and I felled many an opponent with it.

*The Straight-leg Roundhouse **one-leg** Sweep Kick*

*The Straight-leg Roundhouse **two-legs** Sweep Kick*

Rear-leg "cutting" version of the kick

Front-leg "cutting" version of the kick

Description

"Cutting" Kicks are technically easy to perform and a regular Straight-leg Roundhouse to a standing leg will be generally enough to provoke a fall. But, as an intended **takedown**, it is better to perform them in the more classic way that we shall describe here: Kick the side/back thigh *in a slightly upwards direction*. The Figure here shows a *comparative top view* of the (**diagonally upward**) Sweep Kick and a regular (**horizontal**) Straight-leg Low Roundhouse Kick.

The Sweep Kick has all the attributes of the regular Straight-leg Roundhouse, and especially the hip twist and full commitment, *but the trajectory, especially after impact is slightly up*, in order to bend the leg at the knee while

This top view shows well that the kick is very much a hybrid between low Straight-leg Roundhouse- and Front- Kicks

lifting it. Of course this Sweep Kick is a fully committed "kick-through" move aiming for another half-meter **through** the leg.

These kicks may seem wishful thinking to some. The author wants to assure the dubious reader that these are pretty easy techniques to score with when mastered, and they were some of my favorites at a certain time in my sporting career. The key is **timing** and, of course, parsimonious and judicious use. The "Low Kick Sweep" works best on opponents that will react backwards to a forward lunge, by closing their stance, elevating their center of gravity and starting the legs moving in a direction your kick will accelerate.

➡️

...A lot of drilling is necessary to develop the "feel" of the kick, especially in free-fighting training, but the result is worth the effort.

The coming Drawings show the delivery of the Kick to the opponent's front leg, after a jab to provoke some leg movement on his part. It is imperative to aim precisely at the upper side of the knee, and then kick *up and through.* Always follow up while he lands down.

Single-leg kick takedown. Follow up

And the next Drawings show in turn the same kick, but delivered to both legs, when your jab has caused him to close his stance even more. Aim for the same spot on his front leg, but with your upper shin this time. Kick *through* with the hips.

The two-legs kick takedown: great against a "runner"

Key points

- Fully committed kick only: kick at least half a meter *through* the leg.
- Strike the *side or back* of the leg only, at upper knee/lower thigh level.
- The Sweep Kick will not work as a takedown on a low-stance stationary opponent. The purpose of the *jab* is to cause the start of a slight retreat that "liberates" the foot from the floor.
- Keep your *guard up*, and always follow up.

Targets

Very specifically the side and back of the knee.

Typical Applications

As mentioned, the typical application of these kicks, -besides the straight orthodox use presented above-, is as 'Cutting' Kicks. As the kicks are nearly simultaneous, the general idea is to kick in a position that allows you to 'smother' the incoming kick while delivering yours. As you attack his standing leg, you will certainly jam his delivery and weaken his kick; but make sure you cover yourself with your arm, or shoulder. ➤

... The coming Figures show an unorthodox *front-leg* application against a Roundhouse Kick: Lean back and control the incoming Roundhouse by buffering it with your shoulder or with your opposite hand, while delivering your own Straight-leg Roundhouse Sweep Kick to his standing leg. Remember to kick *through and up*. You can also hop slightly forward during delivery to further jam his expected range.

Front-leg Cutting Kick

And the next Figures show the same technique, but delivered with the *rear leg*. This one will work better if you start with a small *angling lunge* to his in-side.

Angling rear-leg cutting Kick

Specific training

The *upward angle* and powerful *kick-through* aspects of this specific Sweep Kick must

be drilled on a heavy bag hanging *with bottom just at knee level*, or on a long bag *hold diagonally* by a partner or a belt. The Drawing shows how you must try to lift and displace the bag *up and laterally* with your kick; but no pushing, just kicking!

Kick diagonally up. A low-hanging fat bag or an obliquely-held long bag will suit the purpose

Self defense

The Figures *at the top of next page* show an aggressive and highly practical version of the Cutting Kick against a rear-leg Roundhouse Kick from opposite stances. The Kick is closely following a *timing*-Stop Punch, which is sometimes a safer tactic. The maneuver will work especially well if you have conditioned your opponent with a few retreats from his rear-leg Roundhouse. You then suddenly stop-reverse-punch him in the middle of his kick development (eventually evading out a bit). The Reverse Punch has the added benefit of pushing him even more off-balance, still with his kicking leg in the air. The rear-leg Straight-leg Roundhouse Sweep Kick to the knee of his standing leg will both damage his joint and take him down harshly. ➤

Timing stop-punch/kick against a rear-leg Roundhouse Kick

And the coming Drawings show a very typical *Kyokushinkai* technique, where leg blocks of 'Low Kicks' are commonplace: You will kick his rear leg after having caused him to lift his front leg! Throw a front-leg Low Kick towards his inner upper thigh or groin to cause him to block by lifting the front leg. Immediately *land deeply forward* while controlling his front hand from the inside, and push back to keep him on his rear leg. Extend your hand forward against his chest and push back more while you deliver the Straight-leg Roundhouse Sweep Kick to the back of his rear leg. Follow up, with an Essential Downward Heel Kick for example.

Provoke his block, keep him on one leg and kick!

Addendum

A related example extracted from our book 'Stop Kicks' will be presented. It is a Near-stop Kick, based on catch-blocking a kick while executing the Roundhouse Stop sweep Kick. The Sweep Kick itself, in the example, is of the front-leg Hopping type.

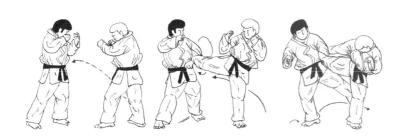

Catch and kick in the same smooth move

And to conclude, we shall present two ground versions of the Roundhouse Sweep Kick, as described in our book about Ground Kicks. The first example is the classic Chinese Iron Broom technique, followed by an Axe Kick. In this example, the Sweep Kick is well delivered according to the same principles we have presented here. In the second example, the Iron Broom has just placed the opponent off-balance, but has not succeeded in taking him down; it will be therefore followed by a Ground Spin-back Hook Sweep Kick.

Iron Broom Ground Roundhouse Sweep kick and Axe Kick follow-up

Iron Broom Sweep Kick followed by Ground Spin-back Hook Sweep Kick to standing leg and Ground Axe Kick finish

I hated every minute of training, but I said, 'Don't quit. Suffer now and live the rest of your life as a champion'.
~Muhammad Ali

9. THE LOW DOWNWARD ROUNDHOUSE KICK

General

This is, again, an *Essential* basic kick, as described in previous work, but delivered to a low target. The parent kick is a surprising technique designed to attack the *head from above*, which is fantastic for point tournaments or as a combination start in full-contact sports. The low version of the Kick, -which trajectory makes it unsuitable to attack knees and thighs-, will generally be used only on a grounded, kneeling or bending opponent. It is an interesting kick though, and very effective in those special situations. This low version is relatively common in Indonesian styles, known for their fierce and realistic maneuvers. It has therefore been seriously battle-tested and is worth drilling.

Description

Please refer to my previous book for a more in-depth analysis of the classic version of

Exaggerate the twist of the Roundhouse chamber and kick down

this *Essential Kick*. In the 'low version', the chambering is lower and less pronounced, but the principles stay the same. See Illustration: Chamber the leg as you would a Full Roundhouse Kick, and then keep pivoting until you have half your back towards the opponent. Extend the leg down, *through* the target, and *chamber back*.

Key points

- This is a snap kick, whipping in and out: You must kick a few inches into the target, but then immediately forcefully *chamber back*.
- *Connect* with ball of foot, upper foot, ankle or lower shin.
- *Turn the hips* fully before you connect.

Targets

Mostly the head and the back of the neck. Between the shoulder blades and the clavicles are also worthy targets.

Typical Applications

As mentioned, this kick is mainly applicable to a leaning or kneeling opponent. The Drawing shows a very practical application of the kick as a follow-up to a successful groin or solar plexus attack. Your first kick has connected with his groin and caused him to bend forward in pain. Lower your leg and deliver a Downward Roundhouse with your other leg, *to the back of his exposed neck*. The back of the neck is a sensitive target and the kick is potentially very dangerous. **Caution is warranted!**

A great combination for self-defense: Groin Kick and Downward Roundhouse when he bends over from pain

The following Figures show the *other classic* practical application of the Kick: A *follow-up to a back-of-the-knee attack*. In this example, you block your opponent Spin-back Back Kick/Backfist combo by evading to his out-side. Control his hand while delivering an Outside-tilted Heel Stomp Kick to the back of his knee. As he falls on his knee and crumples forward, deliver your Downward Roundhouse to the back of his neck. Again, be careful!

Back-of-the-knee Stomp to force him to kneel, then Downward Roundhouse

Specific training

Make sure you drill the kick at different heights. Drill the kick on a standing bag, a lying bag, a focus pad on a chair, a pile of judo mats or a tire held by a partner.
It is also important to drill the **kick-through feel** on a pad hold by a partner, as shown in the Photos at the top of next page.

Drill at all heights on the standing bag

The old tire is always a great drilling tool

A focus pad on a chair and a pile of training mats will make great targets at different heights

Nothing like a partner for a good drill and the feeling of the kick going through

Self defense

The next Figures show the use of the Kick *after an arm-lock has brought your opponent on his knees*. In this instance, you evade a punch on your assailant's out-side while controlling his attacking hand and getting hold of it. You can soften him with a simultaneous palm strike. Bring him down on one knee with an elbow lock, and push him down while starting the delivery of your Downward Roundhouse. The kick "helps" him down and should be delivered in a non-snap and heavier manner, in order to bring his head all the way to the floor. As soon as the head reaches the floor, you could switch your stance to hit his head with a downward knee strike from the other leg.

An arm-lock push will bring him into perfect position for the Downward Roundhouse Kick

3   4   5   6

Another good move to achieve the necessary bent-over position for this kick is the knee strike to the groin or to the solar plexus, as will now be shown.

➤

... The next Figures show a great combination ending with the kick, again, to the back of the neck. You block an incoming punch in a Cross-block (*Juji uke – Karatedo*) and you deflect it to your opponent's in-side. You then slap the arm down with the front hand to allow for a Palm Strike to the face. Keep control of your opponent's arm to allow for a circular Elbow Strike to his face, while you put him off-balance forward with a quick small Sweep. Follow up with a Knee Strike to his abdomen as you release the arm and catch the back of his neck. Pivot back to leave the space in front of him empty as you push down his neck or pull on his arm. As he bends over or stumbles to the floor, kick down to the exposed back neck.

The kick is highly suitable as a follow-up to a circular knee to the solar plexus

Illustrative Photos

Simple Downward Roundhouse Kick to the thigh of a bent leg – **Roy Faige**

The basic Essential high Downward Roundhouse Kick on the standing focus bag

*The **high** basic Downward Roundhouse Kick in action – Marc de Bremaeker; view from both sides*

*The **low** Downward Roundhouse Kick drilled on the focus pad*

The Hand-on-floor version of the Downward Roundhouse Kick

The will to win, the desire to succeed, the urge to reach your full potential... these are the keys that will unlock the door to personal excellence.
~Confucius

10. THE LOW HOOK KICK

General

The Low Hook Kick is not a very powerful kick, and therefore must be directed as precisely as possible to sensitive points, like the knee itself or the nerve endings on the side of the thigh. It is fast though, and generally coming at an unexpected angle; it therefore can be very useful as part of a combination. The kick is generally delivered with the *front leg*, fast and explosively, as speed is its main attribute. A rear-leg delivery would be more part of a feint kick, and would rely more on deception than on speed. The Kick is, in my personal opinion, a great offensive opening move, fast and very safe; it can painfully draw an opponent's attention away from a subsequent more powerful attack. My personal favorite combination is a *Low* Hook Kick attack to the outside of an opponent's front knee, followed by a *high* Head Roundhouse Kick coming from his in-side (See Photos). Drill the Low Hook Kick to make it a painful move, and your combination will work all the better.

The painful low-outside Hook Kick clears the way for the high-inside Downward Roundhouse

Description

Lacking power, the classical Low Hook Kick is generally practiced **dynamically**, with a front hop. The Photos show the classic straight-leg delivery, fully in line with an Essential basic front-leg Hook Kick. There is always some "**hooking**" to be given into the target after impact. For the basic theory about Hook Kicks and the principles of "hooking" at impact into the target, the reader is invited to refer to previous treatises about *Essential Kicking*.

The classic front-leg Low straight-leg Hook Kick

...The following Figure shows a *bent-leg* **chambering** version of the Kick, not to be confused with the *bent-leg* **finish** of the hooked version of the Hook Kick. This is different and more of a low kick version of the basic Curved Side Kick. It is confusing to the opponent and is also a more powerful kick at impact though; and therefore, quite useful. For clarity, we have included an illustration of the classic straight-leg version to compare to.

*The **bent-leg** chambering version of the kick*

*The basic **straight-leg** Low Hook Kick, for comparison*

Key points

- Keep the upper body as immobile as possible to *avoid telegraphing your kick*. This must be a fast and deceptive maneuver (Also refer to 'Stealth Kicks').
- Always kick *through* the target, and then add some **hooking** by bending the leg through the target.
- When attacking the side and rear of the leg, do not fall into the trap of considering this as a sweep: Even when aiming to cause your opponent to fall, it is always a *kick first*.

Targets

The knee from all sides, the inner and outer mid-thigh, the groin, the ankle, the base of the calf.

Typical Applications

The Photos show the use of the Kick in a *clinching* situation, where all low kicks are relevant. Aim for the ankle or the base of the calf. This is generally not enough, and you will have to follow up with other Low Kicks.

Low Hook Kick in clinching situation; keep kicking

... The next Photos show a classic use of the kick as a *combination opener* in which you hit your opponent's knee for pain and misdirection, and to put him somewhat off-balance. As shown, from same stances, you attack his front knee from the outside and then lower the attacking leg deep forward. Then spin-back into a high Spin-back Hook Kick with your other leg. This is a typical **Low outside/High inside** combination.

Low Hook on one side, high Hook on the other

and...View from the other side

And the Figures show the application of the *front-leg kick* as a classic takedown in opposite stances, after a fake jab turning into grab. Remember: This is a **Kick,** *not* a sweep. The end result is the same, but more painfully so! Aim for the knee. Follow up with a punch and a stomp for example.

Hook-kick the knee while pushing him forward: both a kick and a takedown

Specific training

The most important aspect of this kick to train is the **explosiveness** of the delivery and the covering of any **tell-tales**. Practice in front of the mirror, and in front of a long heavy bag. Then practice combinations based on a Low Hook Kick opening, with no preceding hand move and no telegraph of your intentions (Refer to '*Stealth Kicks*'). Invest time in serious **Plyo-Flex** training: this Kick can be drilled to become surprisingly powerful, and it is work well-spent. Reminder: **Low Kicks require serious drilling!**

Self defense

The following Photos show the use of the Kick as the finishing touch of a defensive combination that switches attacks from side to side. If an assailant grabs your shoulder from behind, you have to take back the initiative quickly, before he follows up and takes control of the situation. In this example, twist back explosively, and use your forearm (Side of the grabbed shoulder) to strike his elbow joint *with breaking it in mind*. This move will also throw his upper body sideways and towards the Uppercut Back Kick (an important basic *Essential Kick*) you will be launching with the leg of the other (non-grabbed) side. You then switch sides again to use your other leg for a powerful *Low Hook Kick* to the side of his knee. In this instance, try to kick as **powerfully** as possible and to aim precisely at the knee joint; this is to be a crippling kick.

The Low Hook Kick as the finishing strike in a release from a rear shoulder grab

The Drawings below show the use of the Kick as a throw or as a pre-throw "softener" in a classical leg-grab situation: You have blocked your assailant's Roundhouse Kick and caught his leg. Attack his face with a palm or fingertips strike, while you start delivering a rear-leg Low Hook **Kick** to the base of his calf. The Kick should hurt him. Follow up smoothly with an inside leg sweep (O Uchi Gari – Judo) in which you lift him to make the fall start *from as high as possible*, with maximum damage in mind.

A painful variation on the O-Uchi-Gari theme

Not needless to add: should your opponent be crouching, kneeling or bent-over, the Low Hook Kick can be used as a head kick just like the basic Essential Hook Kick. The coming Photos show how a low "**hooking**" Roundhouse Kick to the inside forward knee can buckle your opponent in the right relative position for such a Low Hook Kick to the head.

A Low Hook Kick to the head as a follow-up to a Low Roundhouse

Illustrative Photos

*Classic **Essential** high Hook Kicks*

*The Hook Kick: **Hooking** into the target at impact*

An evading version of the Essential Hook Kick

*The **ground** version of the Low Hook Kick*

Addendum

We shall add here an applied Feint Kick version of the Low Hook Kick, extracted from 'Stealth Kicks'. The point of this example is also to remind the reader of the importance of targeting the groin when justified.

As mentioned more than once, the Hook Kick is not a powerful kick and is usually reserved for targeting the head, preferably in a surprising way for more effect. Versions aiming at lower targets, like the Low Hook Kick described here, are more anecdotic kicks used to divert attention and to allow for further attacks; or they are part of takedown moves. The only exception to this rule is, understandably, the **groin**. This area is the most sensitive of the male body, and is always a prime target. Feinting a mid-level Front Kick, and turning it into a groin Hook Kick will therefore be a very strong move. Executing the Hook Kick at groin level should be done with a slightly bent leg 'hooking' into the groin.

The example we shall present is a Feint Kick against a 'timing' counter-punching opponent. The following maneuver is relevant whether or not you have conditioned the opponent with preparatory Front Kicks. As you chamber the feinting Front Kick, the opponent does not retreat or does not prepare to block, but he initiates a counterpunch at mid-level. This is the most classic Shotokan Karate stop-punching maneuver. By pivoting immediately from a Front to a Hook Kick chamber, you will simultaneously block his incoming attack with your knee; this is reminiscent of many *Stop Kicks* described in our previous book to which the reader is invited to refer. From this position, the short *groin* Hook Kick will be fast and easy. The follow-up illustrated is a full-powered rear-leg Crescent kick to the head, and a classic *Kibisu Gaeshi Ju-Jitsu* Takedown (One-leg Lift).

Application of the feinting Front-chambered **groin** *Hook Kick*

11. THE LOW SPIN-BACK HOOK KICK

General

The Low Spin-back Hook Kick is obviously the spin-back version of the previous kick, and all what was said before is relevant here again. But the Spin-back version is much more powerful though, because of the kinetic energy gathered when pivoting. It is therefore a more practical and efficient technique.

This Kick is also a great Sweep Kick against the standing leg of a kicking opponent, as illustrated by the *ground* or *Drop* version of the Kick in the Photos.

All in all, the Low Spin-back Hook Kick is an easy-to use and painful kick that can be implemented in many situations.

The Drop version of the Spin-back Hook Kick as the "cutting" takedown of a high kicker – Ziv Faige

Description

The Spin-back Low Kick is identical in its delivery to the Essential classical Spin-back Hook Kick as performed on higher targets and as presented in previous work. As shown in the Illustrations, you spin back, *starting with the head and shoulders*, then hips, and only *last*, the coiled leg. The Kick can be delivered nearly straight and upright, or leaning back, or even with the hand on the floor.

Full Spin-back, just like the Essential high kick, but aiming at the lower leg

Leaning back during the kick will keep your upper body out-of-trouble

You can even lean until your hand touches the floor

...We should also mention, again, the drop version of the kick, generally a "Cutting" Kick or a Low Kick aimed at the groin.

*The Drop Spin-back Low Hook Kick as an **offensive** "cutting" kick*

All variations of the Essential Hook Kicks are valid for the Low Kicks. The reader is invited to refer to the "*Essential Kicks*" volume where a whole chapter is dedicated to Hook Kicks. The reader should also refer to the variations presented in the previous section (Low Hook Kick). For example, - just like the regular Low Hook Kick just presented-, the Spin-back version can be delivered with a slightly bent attacking leg during the spin-back (although that slightly reduces the power of the kick).

Key points

- Release the kicking leg *at the last possible moment* of your pivot, just as a coiled elastic band.
- Kick *through* the target.
- Always add some "*hooking*" at impact by starting to bend back the leg into the target.

Typical Applications

The Figures show an interesting application that underlines the versatility of Low Kicks. It shows the use of the Kick after evading, blocking and deflecting a Side Kick from the outside. Step further behind your opponent and hit his back neck (*high*) with a knife-hand strike. Then, spin-back to deliver a *low* Hook Kick to the side of his front knee. Follow up, with a *high* back-fist strike for example.

A low Spin-back Hook Kick is painful and surprising, especially in-between high strikes

One of the most common uses of this Kick in traditional and sport *Karate* is as a counter to sweeps. In these cases, the Kick is used as a sweeping take-down itself, but more often than not it is a **real kick**, disguised as a sweep if the rules forbid Low Kicks. The first Figures below show how to evade a sweep, by lifting the attacked leg and then lowering it back into your own sweep-kick of the sweeping leg. You then follow up with a Spin-back Low Hook Kick to the sweeping leg of your now-off-balance opponent.

Lift the leg and sweep the sweep; then kick

The next Figures show the other approach against a sweep: You go *with the sweep* and so cause your opponent to overstretch, while you start your spin-back.

Do not resist, go with the sweep; then spin-back hook kick

The Photos will show an *aggressive* hi/hi/lo combination. Lunge forward with a Reverse Punch (*Gyacku Tsuki – Karatedo*) towards your opponent's face, naturally followed (*hip pull*) by a high rear-leg full-powered Roundhouse Kick. Lower the leg while keeping the circular momentum, and spin back into the Low Hook Kick to the side of his front thigh.

Unexpected: Hi Cross punch, Hi Roundhouse Kick, Lo Spin-back Hook Kick

The coming Figures show, again, the use of the Kick in an outside evasion maneuver, this time blocking a full-step Punch (*Oie Tsuki – Karate*). Keep pivoting directly into the Spin-back Kick to the side or back of his front leg. Lower the leg and complete the pivot into a full-powered high Roundhouse Kick with the other leg. You could also roundhouse-kick low, in the spirit of the book, but the author has already made clear that he tends to prefer alternating heights in combinations, and advises getting used to it in training.

Evade out and turn the evasion into a Spin-back Kick

Specific training

- This Kick needs *precision* drilling as it needs to be fast and accurate. Drill on a marked long heavy bag, delivering the kick upright and bent-over, and from different ranges.
- Hit a *tire* hold by a partner (See Figure).

Drill on the old tire for speed, power, accuracy and penetration

Self defense

The next Photos show a very simple maneuver, to be used when suddenly punched. As your assailant jabs towards your face, you lean back while stop-kicking him with a front-leg Side Kick to the knee. Keeping your upper body away, you lower the leg and spin back into a Hook Kick to the side of the same knee.

*Low Stop-Side Kick followed by Spin-back Hook to **same** knee*

And the next Drawings show the Kick as a natural follow-up of a spin-back maneuver: As an assailant grabs your wrist with his opposite hand, you spin back around the axis of your front foot/grabbed wrist while lifting the hand and bending the elbow. You classically liberate your wrist by pulling it free in the opening between his thumb and other fingers. Complete the spin-back with a Low Hook Kick to his rear leg. Follow up in a manner adapted to what the situation warrants.

Any spin-back pivot can be capped with the Spin-back Hook Kick

Illustrative Photos

The classic Spin-back Hook Kick in combat – **Marc De Bremaeker**

Drilling the Essential high Spin-back Hook Kick

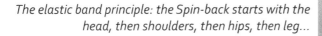

The elastic band principle: the Spin-back starts with the head, then shoulders, then hips, then leg...

Addendum

We shall just add here an applied version of the Kick extracted from 'Stop Kicks'. It is a Cutting Stop Kick version executed upwards to cause a hard takedown, a technique typical of *Yoseikan Budo*. The Drawings are quite self-explanatory.

High-takedown Spin-back Hook Cutting Kick against Front kick attack

THE LOW SPIN-BACK HOOK KICK 109

12. THE LOW SIDE KICK

Yoko Fumikiri (Karatedo)

General

This is a devastating kick, ideal for self-defense, safe to deliver and extremely effective. It is reportedly the kick of choice of *Bruce Lee's Jeet Kune Do* system, advocating the attack of the foremost point of the opponent with the forward weapon closest to him (Front-leg Kick). It can be delivered fast from the guard position and it gives maximum results for minimum effort. It is *not* a Stomp though, but a regular kick with chambering and chambering-back. This is a must-practice kick, in all schools and all systems. It is often a front-leg kick, used as a **stop-kick** in all situations or as a "**cutting**" kick against the standing leg of a kicking adversary. It can easily be delivered while leaning safely back, which adds to its safety. Given the ease of execution and the sensitivity of the knee as a target, it is probably one of the best self-defense kicks available!

Fumikiri – Low Side Kick by Oren Faige

A great self-defense kick in all its forms: front- or rear-leg, body-bent, hand-on-floor, hopping, and more...

*Classic **Krav Maga** series: Wrist grab-release concluded by a Low Side Kick to the knee*

Description

The classic Kick is an *Essential* Penetrating Side Kick delivered to the legs of the opponent. But all variations of the classic Side Kick are applicable to the Low Side Kick. Our previous book about *Essential Kicks* contains a whole Chapter about Side Kicks, and the reader is invited to refer to it for the general theory of optimal execution. As discussed in the introduction, the amount of chambering for the low version will depend on the situation, **but some chambering is definitely needed**: the kick is delivered with the classic *hip thrust* of the classical Side Kick, which gives it its tremendous power. Some *recoiling back* is needed as well, after penetrating the target a bit.

The first set of Illustrations shows the classic delivery of the kick *from the front leg*. The upper body can be bent back as much as needed to keep it away from the opponent.

The second set shows a version of the Essential *Upward* Side Kick applied to the low "gate". In Japanese, it would be a '**Keage**' version, as opposed to the classic penetrating '**Kekomi**' version. This is a kick to use fast when you are too close for the classic Penetrating Low Side Kick: It is much less powerful as it supposes less chambering, but it is *faster* and still painful on the shins. Follow-up is definitely required though.

Front-leg Low Side Kick. Make sure you chamber back

*The more '**Keage**' version of the kick: faster but less powerful*

Key points

- *Avoid telegraphing* your kick by moving the upper body in any way.
- *Explode* into the kick, and if you need to cover distance, hop after chambering the kick for minimum telegraphing.
- Always *chamber* in and back.

Targets

The knee from all sides, the shins, the thigh and even the hip and groin area.

Typical Applications

As mentioned before and illustrated by the coming Photos, this is a great *Cutting Kick*: side-kick the standing leg of your opponent as he attempts a rear-leg high Roundhouse Kick. Make sure you are ready to smother your opponent's own Kick with your shoulder and guard if needed. This technique is a basic codified exercise of the *Sankukai* style of *Karate* already mentioned, part of their 'Randori ni no Kata'.

The "cutting" version of the Low Side Kick

But, as illustrated by the following Figures, this is also the kick of choice when you find yourself on your opponent's *out-side*. In the offensive combination presented, you throw a **high** Reverse Punch/rear-leg **midsection** Front Kick, and you leave your hand in front of his face for vision-jamming. Land deep on his *out-side* while striking his face from the in-side with your palm. Try to keep control of his blocking front hand while delivering a Side Kick to the out-side or to the back of his knee.

The kick of choice if you can get to your opponent's out-side

And this is also the kick of choice to *safely close the gap* with your opponent or to stop him at the slightest hint of movement, as shown in the Photo. Such an un-telegraphed Kick will help you close the gap, will hurt your opponent, and will prevent him from any counterattack. Remember to **keep upper body immobile** as you hop into the Kick.

Low front-leg Side Kick as a stop-kick

The next Photos show a typical combination starting with this *gap-closing version of the kick*. Once the kick executed and the gap closed, you can then extend your front hand

when landing forward in order to cause him to block, and take control of his arm. Pull the arm in, while delivering a cross to his jaw from very much out of his vision range. Finish with a "Low Kick".

Close the gap with the front-leg Low Side Kick as it will immobilize your opponent; follow up

The next Figures show an interesting, slightly exotic, variation of the Kick: A *rear-leg kick delivery* and attacking the opponent's **rear** knee! In this example, you evade a Jab forward and to your opponent's *in-side* while reverse-punching him (Keep your other

hand up!). Immediately keep pivoting with the hips to deliver a Side Kick to his rear knee, as his front one is too close in range.

Rear-leg Penetrating Side Kick to opponent's rear knee

Specific training

- This is a Kick which needs to be drilled for power: practice on a *standing bag* held by a partner. Make sure you *explode* into the movement. **Low Kicks require training!**
- Practice on a *tire* hold by a partner for penetration.
- Practice for "non-telegraphing" in front of the *mirror*.
- Practice closing the gap against a *partner* with protected legs: He will try to stop-hit you, or retreat; you must explode into the Kick with no tell-tales.
- Improve your abilities with regular and comprehensive *PLYO –FLEX* training.

Self defense

The Drawings show the classic use of the rear-leg Kick to the standing knee of a kicking opponent, whose leg you have caught from the inside. This is a **Kick**, not a throw, but it will get him on the floor all the more. Immediately stomp his ankle to neutralize him.

The classic rear-leg Cutting Kick

And the coming Photos show another example of Cutting Kick, this time after a *Catching Block* from the outside. It will be followed by countering with a front-leg Side Kick to the upper thigh, in the groin area. In this specific case, it is more effective to use a hybrid of the *Penetrating-* and of the *Upward-* Side Kick.

The Side Kick to the upper thigh reverberates to the groin area!

The next Figures show a self-defense application of the Kick at *lower shin/ankle level:* You are grabbed at the collar from behind and pushed forward. Make one step forward to neutralize the push, and start to pivot, so that he pushes in the void. Side-kick his ankle and knife-hand his elbow joint. Keep the pivot and conclude with a straight-leg Roundhouse ('Low Kick') to the knee with the other leg. {You could *also* pivot back in the other direction and deliver an Essential Short Back Kick to his abdomen – not illustrated}.

Yield to his push to put him off-balance and bounce back with a Low Side Kick to the shin

As mentioned already, this is the Kick of choice when you succeed in positioning yourself on your opponent's **out-side** (his blind side). It will also allow you to set-up a good follow-up. The Photos show an outside evasion against a high Punch with a 'Block & Catch', and a simultaneous *Small Roundhouse Kick* to the groin. The leg recoils and goes directly (not touching the floor!) into a Side Kick to the side of his leg. This is a classical combination, very natural in its execution and which should be drilled as such. You can follow up by pulling his arm forward while stepping behind him and placing him in a rear naked choke (*Hadaka Jime – Judo*). You can also stomp-kick the back of his other knee for more control.

From inside Roundhouse to outside Side Kick

And the following Drawings show the same *gap-closing technique*, to start an offensive combination, just as presented in the "Typical Application" section. But, this time, the maneuver has the real purpose of getting control of the opponent with an Arm-lock.

Close the gap with a Low front-leg Side Kick; attack his eyes to cause a block and get hold of his arm from the outside; proceed to arm-lock

Illustrative Photos

The Low Side Kick – Roy Faige

The Essential Upward Side Kick – Ziv Faige

The Essential Spin-back Side Kick

The Essential Penetrating Side Kick

Addendum

The Low Side Kick is a fantastic **Stop Kick,** as mentioned many times. It stars in our book treating the subject and here are two applied examples extracted from it.

Minimal-chamber front-leg Hopping Side Stop Kick

Front-leg Hopping 'Obstruction' Low Side Stop Kick; against an opponent starting is own full-powered Hopping Kick and expecting you to retreat

The Side Kick targeting the lower part of the opponent's body can, of course, be delivered from the ground. Here are two examples, among many, extracted from **Ground Kicks**. The first is the simply the ground version of the 'Obstruction' Stop Kick. The second will be a follow-up Kick to the back of the standing opponent's knee.

Ground Side Stop Kick to the knee of a kick being chambered

Present your knee as an easy target, but as a trap. Evade the expected kick down and use the opponent's momentum to attack his kicking leg. First a Ground Roundhouse will hurt and further his momentum, then a Ground Side Kick will hurt him more and hopefully take him down

Extracted from **Stealth Kicks**, we have chosen to present a <u>misdirecting</u> *Feint Kick* in context: the ***Roundhouse-chambered Low Side Kick.*** The Photos are self-explanatory.

You condition your opponent with a few high Roundhouse Kicks. The Feint Kick will be chambered in the same way, but will develop from the misdirecting chamber as a Low Side Kick

13. THE LOW SIDE STOMP KICK

Yoko Fumikomi (Karatedo)

General

The name of the Kick makes it self-explanatory: A Downward Low Side Kick *crushing* the top of the opponent's foot or the back of his knee, and stomping it *into* the floor. This is a devastating kick, of course, painful to the extreme and easy to deliver. Just remember to keep your guard up as it brings you pretty close to your opponent! It is interesting to note that this Kick, often as a natural follow-up to the *Full Essential Crescent Kick*, is very common in old traditional *Shotokan-ryu Karatedo* Forms.
The reader should note that the examples given in the previous section, about *Low Side Kicks*, are often partly "stomping" in their delivery. We have presented purposely two sections for Low Side Kicks: regular and stomp; but it is clear that most deliveries in Martial Arts are hybrids with more or less emphasis, and that only classification needs make for the description of the classic extremes. Some of the kicks presented here in the Applications can be found by the reader less "stomping" than some from the previous section. And vice-versa... We are only asking you to understand the principles and work as per your affinities and as per the specific situation.

Classic Krav Maga series: The use of the Low Side Stomp Kick

Excerpt of Heian Godan Kata form:
Crescent Kick turns into Side Stomp Kick

Another classic Krav Maga series: side knee Stomp

Description

As shown in the Figure, this Kick *definitely* requires **chambering**, very much like a regular Side Kick. The amount of chambering is up to the circumstances. Once chambered, you then stomp *through* the target, as if you were trying to hit the floor as powerfully as possible. In this kick-type, you do not chamber back automatically: You can either grind your opponent's joint into the floor, or remove your leg to follow up. Please note than if you push powerfully an opponent backwards while keeping your foot on his, he will fall down in a nasty way.

The Photos show the classical delivery of the Kick as an intrinsic part of a crescent kick, just as practiced in traditional Karate Kata forms: Hit your opponent's guard with a high Crescent Kick and stomp down on his lead foot, as if to crush it *into* the ground.

The rear-leg simple delivery of the Stomp Side Kick

The Crescent Kick into the guard turns into a Side Stomp Kick

Key points

- This Kick, in its orthodox form, is different from the previous Low Kick: You kick *through* without any chambering-back afterthought. Whether you kick the foot, ankle or back of the knee, the feeling is *total stomping*, as if trying to kill a crawling insect as forcefully as possible. This is the ultimate "kick-through".
- Keep your *guard up*.
- Always *chamber* up: stomping is about power.

Targets

The top of the foot, the ankle and the back of the knee.
Any part of a lying opponent, but preferably the ankles and fingers.

Typical Applications

The next Figures show an important and quite common application, which principle we have already encountered with other kicks: The "**Scrape and Stomp**". After a distance-closing Low Side Kick to the knee (or a Stop Kick), do not chamber back; it will make your kick less powerful and sort of a "pushing" kick. *But* you then start switching your body weight to the kicking leg, while *scraping* down his shin to finish up in a *stomp* of the top of his foot. The aggressive scraping of the sensitive tibia (shin bone) is intended to be a painful addition to the Stomp. Of course, keep your guard up ,and then follow up. It is less powerful a Stomp, but has an annoying and potentially debilitating *grating* effect.

The cunning Scrape & Stomp

And the next Figures show the application of the Side Stomp Kick in a **Clinching** situation. Simple but effective, and therefore always the best application. Please note that some *scraping* is also possible in these close quarters, even if you have chambered up: Just make sure you kick down as close as possible to the shin, and, hopefully, some scraping will occur.

Side Stomp Kick as soon as clinched

The coming Figures at the top of next page show the application of the Kick as a *"Cutting" Kick* against the standing leg of a kicking opponent. This Kick is different from the previous regular Cutting Low Side Kick: In this particular case, you will stomp into the back of the knee to bring his knee *into* the floor and *grind* it in. In the example, you avoid a high Roundhouse Kick to the head by bending and leaning back, and then you immediately hop into a Side Stomp Kick to the back of his knee; in fact as soon as his leg has passed you over. Be **careful**: This is a very dangerous technique for your opponent's knee joint. But in a *serious real-life encounter*, grind his knee joint into the floor, as if it was a cigarette butt.

Duck the high Roundhouse and side-stomp the back of the standing knee

Specific training

Although it seems simple and easy, this Kick still needs serious training for power and "through"-kicking: Practice on a tire hold by a partner (knee-like target) and lying on the floor (ankle-like target, see Illustration). Practice the scrape and stomp on a heavy bag and a focus pad lying on the floor (illustrated). Practice on a human-form-bag hold by a partner or a bag lying on the floor. All Low Kicks need training, just like regular Kicks: the Stomp is no exception!

Scrape and Stomp-training; use a bag and a focus pad

Stomp the old tire for power; think about crushing it

Self defense

3rd party ✓

As shown in the Figures, this Kick, delivered to the back of the knee, is the best maneuver to *help a third party* being aggressed: Coming from behind the assailant, grip his shoulder while stomping the back of his knee into the floor. Executed with power, this maneuver will immediately neutralize any threat, and even a punch in mid-flight. From there, you can follow up with an arm-lock, a choke or a strike to the head. You will have protected from harm your loved ones or a helpless victim.

Best Kick to help a third party

Just as we have seen with the *regular* Low Side Kick, the Stomp Side Kick is a natural follow-up to a Groin Roundhouse delivered from the out-side of an opponent. This combination presented in the Figures below, is different than the similar combination presented in the previous section, as the kick to the knee is a **Stomp** all the way down. In the example, you evade and control your assailant's punch from the *outside*, catch his arm and deliver a fast Groin Small Roundhouse Kick (from the out-side). Chamber back, and from the chambered position, stomp directly down into the back of his knee. Keep control of his arm, catch his hair to pull back his head and open his throat to a knife-hand strike or an elbow strike, if warranted. This whole combination is an extremely devastative technique, on account of hitting the groin and crushing the knee.

Groin Roundhouse Kick to Side Stomp Kick to the back-of-the-knee. An all-the-way Stomp will allow for dangerous follow-ups

The Drawings coming at the top of next page show the use of the **Scrape & Stomp** version of the Kick in a release technique from a Front Choke when pinned against a wall. Contract your neck muscles, lift one arm as high as possible to immobilize one of his choking hands and deliver a fast *Essential Lift Kick* to his groin. Start immediately to pivot forcefully, keeping your arm up in order to lock his wrist, and let your Lift Kick *turn naturally into a high Side Stomp Kick-chamber.* Deliver the **Scrape-and-Stomp Side Kick** to his foot top, while lowering your arm forcefully into his grip, downward elbow strike-style. Keep your foot on his stomped foot, get control of his releasing arms and deliver a side elbow strike to his face. Follow up if necessary. ➡

Groin kick into Scrape & Stomp Side Kick; all in a choke release technique

The next Figures now show a classic application against a typical traditional *Kung-Fu* type Sweep/Foot Catch that hooks around the front ankle. The Stomp Side Kick is the perfect counter-attack. You neutralize the Sweep by placing all your weight forcefully onto the front foot and get into a Side Kick-chamber with the rear leg. Stomp onto the side of his knee, his leg being stuck in place by yours. When drilling, do not stomp all the way down: This is a grave joint attack to be practiced very **carefully**.

Stomp on an attempted hooking sweep

The next Drawings, at the top of next page, show an example of the use of the side *"Scrape & Stomp"* against a forward *Neck Lock*, "Guillotine"-type. This is a very serious attack which requires an immediate response: Grip his arms to release the pressure, all the while delivering a low version of the *Essential Front Side Kick* to his knee. Pivot slightly while pulling on his arms and turn into a powerful **Scrape & Stomp.** Pivot, straighten up and try to break his hold while *grinding* his ankle *into* the floor. Complete your pivot and get him into an Arm-lock. A great and damaging follow-up would be to get him to the floor by jumping (*Yoko Ukemi*-style) with all your bodyweight on his arm-locked elbow.

Guillotine-release after a "softening" Side Scrape-and-Stomp Kick

And the next Figures show a modern application of the traditional Crescent Kick/Stomp Kick combination. In the example, you *block and catch* your opponent's Jab to pull down on his arm while delivering a full-powered rear-leg Crescent Kick to his head. This will place him sideways and naturally present the back of his knee to the Stomp. This is very dangerous for the knee joint, as the Kick does not come straight from behind, but slightly to the side. **Extreme caution is warranted**, especially in training.

Crescent Kick into Side Stomp

The next Drawings show, again, a *Cutting Kick*, but, this time, it is in order to underline its follow-up. A lingering Stomp allows you to painfully immobilize an opponent while you execute a control technique, in this example an Ankle-lock. Your assailant launches a Side Kick that you evade back by pulling the front leg rearwards, in the spirit of *Shorinji-Kempo's Hiki-Mi* mentioned in the introduction. But, as you **block and catch** the kicking leg, your retreating leg bounces back forward into Side Kick-chamber. You then stomp-kick the back of his knee, while keeping control of his kicking leg. Drive his knee joint into the floor, *drill it in place* and execute a painful twisting Ankle-lock on his other leg. **Be very careful in practice!**

Keep the painful Stomp on for control techniques

Last but certainly not least, the next Photos show a variation of the Kick in which the trajectory is slightly **curved** in order to catch the *side* of your opponent's knee that you are facing. The principle is similar to that of the "Curved Side Kick" mentioned in our book about *Essential Kicks* and it is further illustrated by a sky-view comparison in the Drawing preceding the Photos. It is kind of a *Feint Kick*, a bit surprising and often quite effective. In this example, it helps to buckle the opponent's knee, in spite of the fact that you come from his front. So it goes: In opposite stances, you evade a rear-leg Front Kick by shuffling backwards just enough to avoid being touched. While your assailant lowers his kicking leg, you lift your front foot and stomp the side of his knee *as he lands*. In order to do that, you'll need to *curve* slightly the trajectory of the Stomp in something akin to a mild Outside Crescent Kick move. Follow up.

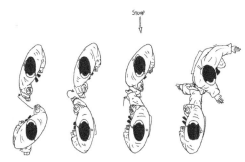

Curve the development of the kick to place it in stomping position

Curve the trajectory to get to the back side of his knee

Illustrative Photos

Low Side Kick on the author by **Mishka Daglietsky**, *restrained by an elastic band for drilling purposes*

Stomping Side Stop-Kick to the hip

Drilling the Stomp Side Kick – **Roy Faige**

Addendum

We have extracted from '**Stop Kicks**' two examples of the use of the fantastic *Side Stomp Kick*, as the finishing follow-up to 'Timing' Stop Kicks. In the first set of Drawings, the Kick flows naturally as the continuation of the Timing Hook Stop Kick which follows a leaning back move to evade from a Jab. The second set of Illustrations shows again the Side Stomp blending seamlessly with the finish of a Crescent Stop Kick which attacked the elbow of a stick-wielding opponent. A Great follow-up Kick indeed!

Evade back, then stop-kick, then stomp

Stop-kick the elbow joint, then stomp-kick the knee joint

From '**Stealth Kicks**', we have extracted an important move from the Chapter treating the *Roundhouse-chambered Side Kick*. As you start a Roundhouse Kick Chamber, your opponent initiates a Counterpunch. Your chamber turns into a **Side Kick** Chamber and therefore into a *Leg Block* of the body punch. From this position, it is easy to stomp the opponent's front ankle. After the *Side Stomp Kick*, you could follow-up with a high Spin-back Hook Kick, as illustrated. Or with anything else for that matter...

Against a counter-puncher: Leg Block to natural Side Stomp and follow-up

The reader surely remembers the '*Stomp & Push*' maneuver described earlier. For the Side Stomp Kick, there is a similar version in which you immobilize the stomped foot while causing the opponent's fall. It is, in this case, a '**Stomp & Pull**', but it is as damaging to the ankle joint. Stomp the opponent's ankle, keep your foot firmly on his with all your weight, and pull him off-balance. In the example, the maneuver is executed offensively: your arm catch also diverts attention from the chamber of the Stomp Kick. **Be careful** in training: it is a joint-damaging technique.

Offensive '**Stomp & Pull**'; *keep your feet crushing his*

14. THE LOW BACK KICK

Ushiro Gedan Geri - Karatedo

General

This is a very simple-to-perform kick, with less hip movement than the corresponding *Essential Penetrating Back Kick*. The low version can be executed with various amounts of chambering and of upper body leaning, as the circumstances dictate. This is a very important Kick for self-defense situations, as, -in real life-, chances of being assailed from behind are unfortunately significant. There are numerous practical variations of the Kick, which main ones will be presented here. Our previous work about "*Essential Kicks*" includes a full chapter about **Back Kicks**: Most of these Essential Back Kicks variations can be delivered *low* as well.

Classic Krav Maga series to release a rear bear hug with a score of Low Back Kicks: Stomp, Donkey kick to shin and Essential Groin Hook Back Kick

Description

The first Figure shows the *classic* delivery of the Kick, just as a regular Back Kick: high chambering and hip penetrating power. Chamber back, of course.

The classic Low Back Kick

But there is a *Stomping* version against a closer opponent (See second Figure), in which there is no chambering back. It will be presented briefly, but separately in a coming section.

The Back Stomp Kick

The third Figure shows a somewhat *Upward* version of the kick (*Keage* in Karatedo), aiming back with a more or less straight leg for the shin or knee of the opponent. No chambering is needed, but the upper body leans forward to stay loosely in a straight line with the kicking leg.

There are other basic variations of the *Essential Back Kick* that can be adapted to the Low Back Kick, like the hooked finish, the uppercut delivery or the spin-back preparation. Some examples of these basic principles will be presented briefly in the Self-defense sub-section.

The Upward straight-leg Low Back Kick

Key points

- Always *chamber up* before kicking.
- Look back *while* kicking: As you are in a precarious position, do not lose time by looking first.

Targets

Knee (See Photo), shins, thigh and groin.

Donkey Kick to the knee

Typical Applications

The Photos show the very useful "*Bent-leg Pendulum*"-variation, often called the
Donkey Kick: As your opponent catches you
with an underarm bear hug from behind, you
take control of his arms and lift the slightly
bent leg forward. You then kick back towards
his shin while bending the leg a little bit more
for added impact. Connect with the heel and
lean forward while kicking.

Low Back Kick to the shin as a rear bear hug-release

The next Photos show a more classic application, including a **Spin-back**. This is a high/
low combination based on luring in a counter-attacking opponent: Launch a high
Reverse Punch to your opponent's face, but immediately switch your weight back
rearwards, lean back and start your Spin-back on the spot. Your upper body is therefore

slipping away from his own eventual
Reverse Punch-counter. You deliver your
Spin-back Back Kick to his front knee,
while keeping your upper body away. A
good follow-up could be a Back-fist strike,
making use of the spinning momentum.

Spin-back Low Back Kick to the knee

The Photos *at the top of next page* show the judicious use of the Kick in a **close combat**
situation: As you are close to the opponent, you jam the power of his possible punches
by rolling into him and smothering him while spinning. All the while, deliver a Spin-back
Circular Downward Elbow Strike to the head. Bend forward to immediately deliver a
Lifting (*Donkey-style*) Back Kick to his unprotected groin. Of course, note that other
Low Back Kicks or Stomp Kicks would do the job as well. Keep kicking to finish him up.

Jam him with an aggressive Spin-back; hit high, then low

Specific training

- Train for power on the standing heavy bag and held-up tire. This is a Power Kick that requires *power training*. Low Kicks require training!
- Train for automatic "*no-peek*"-delivery on the standing bag and tire. No telegraph!
- Work with a *partner* is always productive (See Photo)

A body shield held by a partner is an excellent drill target

Self-defense

The next Photos show the classic **Spin-back Back Kick** to the opponent's *groin*, after a Shin Block of his own "Low Kick". Finish off with an Elbow Strike.

Spin back into Low Back Kick and elbow strike

The **Spin-back** variation is extremely powerful and useful in all kinds of situations.

Another example, in which the *spin starts as a Low Roundhouse* attack, is presented in the coming Photos: Kick *through* with a Low Roundhouse and spin-back into the Low Back Kick.

A Low Roundhouse through the inside front knee will allow you to start your spin-back while the opponent is off-balance, both physically and mentally

And the Essential **Uppercut** version of the Kick is presented in the next Photos, as a 'Timing' groin-stop of a high kicker.

The Uppercut Back Kick comes straight up to the target

A classic **offensive** example of the Essential **Hooked** version of the Back Kick is

presented in the next Photos. A Cross-step Back-fist/Spin-back Back-fist combination places you in the sweet spot for a *Hooking Back Kick* between your opponent's legs.

The Kick goes up, then hooks back forwards

And a **defensive** example is presented in these Photos: Evade a Front Kick by going forward-and-out, and *hop* into a *Hooking Back Kick* between your assailant's legs, **from behind.**

Evade forward and out for the perfect starting position

The Essential **Back Ghost Lift Kick** is a deceptive maneuver delivered with the body turning away *as if you were fleeing* your assailant. It simply lifts fast and unexpectedly, but without power, into the opponent's groin. The Photos show how it is delivered **offensively** after a high punching feint.

The unexpected Back Ghost Lift Kick

The coming Figures show an application of the "**Donkey Kick**" variation in an *Aiki-jitsu* technique against an opponent grabbing both your wrists from behind (*Ushiro Ryote Tori* attack). In fact, the Kick will serve as a softener to ease the execution of the classic Aikido's *Juji Nage* Throw. Kick back with a *Donkey Kick* to his knee or shin and lower the leg onto his foot in a *Back Stomp Kick*. Pivot in between his arms and perform the "self-inflicted" Arm-lock that turns into an easy Throw.

Back Kick and Back Stomp as the start of a rear wrists hold-release

The next Figures show the use of a <u>hooked</u> variation of the **Donkey Kick**, against another rear attack. The finishing touch of the technique will be, again, a crossed-arm self-inflicted Arm-lock Throw. As your assailant grabs your wrist from behind while trying to choke you with his other arm (Aikido's formal *Kubishime* Attack), catch his choking elbow immediately to relieve the pressure. Then, lift your other arm to the side while stepping sideways and forwards. This move can be accompanied by a *Buttocks' Strike* to the opponent's general groin area. Deliver an *Upward Bent-leg Back Kick* to his groin, while "**hooking**" into the target. Lift your grabbed arm over your head and grab his grabbing hand with your other hand. Go down into *Ju-jitsu* Hip Throw position close to your opponent and perform the dangerous Arm-locked Shoulder Throw.

Groin Hooking Back Kick to loosen an assailant's grip

The next Figures show another application of the **Groin Back Kick,** but from further away; it is therefore less of a *Hooked* Back Kick and more of an *Uppercut* Back Kick (See *Essential Book of Martial Arts Kicks*). As your assailant grabs your collar from behind and pushes forward, you do *not* resist. Step and lean forward to put him off-balance, and suddenly kick back towards his groin. Pivot energetically to the outside of his grabbing arm and hit the elbow joint with your forearm. Think of breaking it!Continue your Spin-back move to take control of his arm and get him into an Arm-lock.

Yield forward and step deep, then kick back

And the next Figures give a last self-defense example with the use of the classic **Penetrating** version of the Kick in a frontal attack situation. As an assailant reaches to choke you from the front with both hands, you retreat while pivoting and lean back, in order to place him off-balance before he can strengthen his hold. Chamber your front leg and Back-kick his front knee. You can follow up with a Spin-back Hook Kick, using the other leg.

Retreat and lean back; then chamber high and kick powerfully through his knee

Addendum

Just as a reminder: the Back Kick is also a great tool on the **ground**. In the example below, the Ground Spin-back Back Kick comes after a Ground Downward Roundhouse Kick, executed immediately as you reach the ground.

15. The Low Back Stomp Kick

General

This is a very simple Kick, already introduced earlier in the treatise (Illustrated in the previous Chapter). It is a simple Stomp, just like the Front- or Side-stomp Kicks, but this time delivered slightly behind you. Therefore, we will just present two detailed applications relevant to MMA and Self-defense, as a general illustration. The Stomping principles remain identical.

Description

Lift your knee up high, and, from this chambering position, stomp **onto and through** your (rear) opponent's upper foot or ankle; *as if crushing a bug*. The Photos show the start of a rear bear hug-release. Possible follow-up techniques will be presented in the Applications.

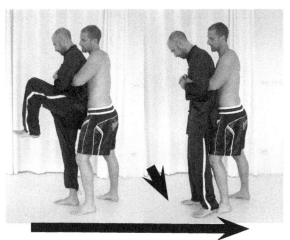

The Back Stomp Kick; chamber high

Typical Application

The Figures below show the Kick used to free yourself from a rear underarm bear hug. It is followed by a classic Takedown release. First chamber high and stomp forcefully on your opponent's foot, placing your stomping foot in the most practical position, usually slightly tilted. Connect with your heel. You can conceivably also scrape your opponent's shin while going down, but it reduces the total energy of the Stomp. Bend immediately forward to grab your opponent's (other) ankle in between your legs. Pull his leg up while pushing him back with your buttocks, to make him fall on his back. Keep hold of his ankle as you immediately back-stomp-kick (again) his exposed groin this time. Note that the whole combination can be preceded by a rear head butt (not illustrated) for further overwhelming the assailant.

Back Stomp Kick, then takedown; then groin Back Stomp

Self defense

The last Figures show another possible finish to the previous technique: after (the rear Head Butt and) the forceful Stomp, you catch the palm of his hand and liberate it down while you pivot. You twist his wrist in a typical *NiKyo* Lock (*Aikido, JuJitsu*) *while kicking his shin* (Low Soccer Front Kick) and completing your pivot. You now use your other hand **to catch his little finger** (pinky) pointing upwards. You bring him down with the *Finger Lock* and can finish him up with further Kicks. Of course, the proficient *AikiJitsuka* could proceed with the classical Nikkyo attack or one of its variations. The "pinky" move is much easier and devastating enough though.

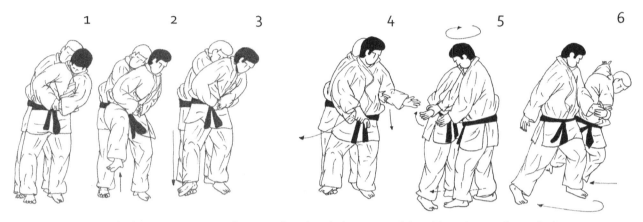

Use the lingering Stomp to free your hand and place a painful and humiliating finger-lock

It does not matter how slowly you go as long as you do not stop.
~Confucius

16. THE HEEL-OUTSIDE LOW KICK

Ha Che Cha Gi (Hapkido), Tendangan Ular Sanca (Pencak Silat)

General

This is a very interesting Kick that is not practiced enough, in my opinion. I have seen variations of this Kick used successfully in very practical Korean, Chinese and Indonesian Arts. It comes at an unexpected angle, and it is pretty powerful **if one takes the time to drill it adequately**. It could be described as a hybrid Crescent Kick/ Downward Heel Kick, with some leg bending and honing onto specific sensitive targets. Although it takes practice to make this Kick efficient and naturally-flowing, it is an important technique for close-quarters situations (See Photos); it definitely should be part of the serious kicker's arsenal for self-defense situations.

A devastating kick to the knee in a clinch situation

Description

The Illustration shows the full-chambered way to deliver the Kick. This is the way to start practicing it, in order to get a feeling of all the components imparting it power. Drill it this way; and only when you have mastered it, you can start to gradually reduce the extent of the chambering both in height and in arc-width. Lift the knee sideways, as if for an *Essential Side Front Kick*, and extend it *high* on your side. Your arm can be inside or outside the leg. You then lower the leg forcefully down and diagonally,

while bending it to get the right range to the target. At the same time you lean sideways with your upper torso to add to the power of the kick. You connect with the heel and kick into the target. The feeling at impact is that of a *hooking* "Donkey Kick". Drilling the kick on a bag is imperative to understand it and to start developing power!

Key points

- Keep your *guard up*: you are close to your opponent.
- *Bend the knee* at the last moment before impact for more power.
- *Keep your upper body immobile* in the first stages of chambering.

Targets

This Kick requires hitting specific sensitive targets only. The side of the knee and of the thigh. The ankle. An interesting variation calls for hitting the kidneys of an opponent in front of you (Illustrated in a Photo in the coming sections), or standing sideways to you. Of course, in opposite sideways stance, the kick can also target the groin.

Some styles of *Pencak Silat* target the back of the calf *from the front*.

Unorthodox targets: Kidneys, groin, calf

Typical Applications

The Photos illustrate the more practical version of the Kick, with less chambering (to

be practiced *only* after you have mastered the classical full delivery). Hitting the knee joint will both be painful and will compromise the opponent's balance.

Fast and efficient: The Heel-outside Low Kick

As mentioned, the Kick can target the **kidneys**, as illustrated in the Photos at the top of next page. Here comes the Photo promised in the 'Targets' section. In our example, the Kick is executed offensively after a Reverse Punch-opening; but this technique is obviously versatile and could be used in numerous other ways.

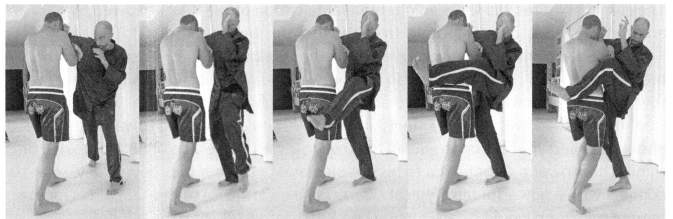

The interesting attack-to-the-back version

The Kick is extremely useful in a *Clinch* situation, as part of, or as the beginning of a combination, in order to take back the advantage. As mentioned before, the Kick is kind of a *hybrid* between a Crescent Kick and a Downward Heel Kick, with a pinch of "Hooking". We shall now show, to allow a more direct comparison, **two** versions of the Kick in the same clinching position: one with *more* and one with *less* "crescent-kick" emphasis. First, the next Figures show the 'Crescent' variation of the Kick. We could have presented this "**Low Crescent Kick**" in a separate Chapter of the book, but this kick is probably only effective enough in this clinching situation where your opponent is grounded by your hold. So, this paragraph will be all we shall say about the 'Low Crescent Kick'.

More a Crescent Kick than a
Heel-outside Kick

And the next Figures, for the sake of completeness, will show, as a comparison, the very effective straighter classic **Heel-outside Low Kick** in the same Clinch. Of course, there are infinite intermediate deliveries in between the Heel-outside Low Kick and the Low Crescent Kick.

The classic Outside-heel Low Kick in a clinch

The coming Figures will show an offensive application of the Kick, followed by an evading step resulting naturally from the foot position after impact. The Kick illustrated is a painful maneuver covering the body movement; it is also a welcome break in the hi/hi/hi punching combo. Pictures will be worth a thousand words. Lunge towards your opponent with a Reverse Punch to the face, and start delivering the Heel-outside Kick with your rear leg. All the while, you are **jabbing towards his eyes** and are leaving your fist up *to limit his field of vision*. Kick the side of his front knee or thigh. Then lower the foot deep to his out-side and twist your hips powerfully, so as to connect with a powerful Jab (Typical *Kizami Tsuki – Karatedo*) to the side of his face. A natural follow-up would be an Outside Leg Reap Throw (*O Soto Gari – Judo*).

The Heel-outside Kick as a facilitator for an evading step

Specific training

As mentioned, this Kick is somewhat unnatural and requires a lot of drilling to become effective and usable in combat. But once mastered, it is surprisingly powerful while coming from a very unexpected angle. It certainly makes it worth the training.

- Work for familiarity and *power* on the heavy bag, both standing and hanging, at different relevant heights.
- Train with a *padded partner* to learn to discern the opportunities of its use.

Drill on the hanging heavy bag and on a bag you hold as you would an opponent

Self defense

Once this technique **becomes natural**, it is very easy to use in any close-combat situation. The fact that the upper body can be bent sideways gives the technique a certain amount of evading qualities. The Figures show how to duck and catch a Jab from the outside, and then follow up with a Hammer-fist Strike to the lower ribs *and a rear-leg Heel-outside Kick to the side of the knee*. Follow up with a full-hipped downward hand Strike to his neck for example (Not illustrated).

Rib strike followed by kick to leg, while leaning out

As we have seen before, these Low Kicks that intrinsically lack power are very useful to help set up Arm-locks, Chokes, Throws or even misdirecting Combinations. The next Figures show the use of the Kick as a painful diversion to allow for the setting of an Arm-lock. In the example, you block a diagonal stick attack to your head by slipping *forward and inside* the strike. Catch and roll your arm over his stick arm while delivering a circular fully-hipped Elbow Strike to his face. Use your rear leg to deliver a Heel-outside Kick to the side/back of his calf/knee, *while setting up the Arm-lock*. Bend back violently to hurt his joint, and then pivot naturally into an underarm hip throw.

The Heel-outside Kick helps setting up a painful arm-lock

The Kick can also be used as the hard "kicking" version of hooking Take-downs. In that case, you execute the technique *with the mind-set of kicking with your heel* into anything coming your way. The first Illustration series shows the **regular** Take-down, while the following one shows the more dangerous **cross-legged** version. Both versions are based on an outside evasion against a punch.

Here comes the first set, that shows the *forward outside* evasion on a Lunge Punch; evasion in which you get control the attacking arm. You then stick to his back and Hook-kick his front leg with your rear while pushing him forward. **Chamber high and kick hard**; follow up as he falls on his face.

The Heel-outside Low Kick as a take-down

And the next series shows the same forward evasion to the outside of his *Reverse* Punch. Get control of his attacking arm and simultaneously strike him, a Palm Strike for example. Hook-kick his forward leg with your rear leg and push him forward. *His legs are crossed and the fall is very dangerous for his knee joint*. Again, if the situation warrants it, chamber high and **kick hard**.

The same dangerous take-down on a crossed-legged opponent

Nobody can make you feel inferior without your consent.
~Eleanor Roosevelt

17. THE ANGULAR KICK TO THE KNEE

General

This is a very practical small kick, not very efficient in itself because it lacks in power, but fantastic as an opener or as an <u>Attrition Kick</u>. It is kind of a hybrid between the Essential angled *"Instep Angular Front Kick"* and the Essential *"Outside Crescent Kick"*; and, of course, delivered at low levels. By **assiduous practice**, the power behind the Kick can be greatly improved, and it becomes a very painful Kick that will surprise many opponents. *Reminder*: Low Kicks require serious drilling!
We will only present one application for this somewhat anecdotic, but still very practical, Kick.

Description

Simply lift the foot into an **Outside Crescent** towards the target, preferably the inside knee. It must be un-telegraphed, and the power of the kick comes from a hip torque at the last moment. Connect to sensitive points only, with the knife edge or the top of the foot, just like for a classic Outside Crescent Kick. The Drawing shows a rear-leg kick, but the principle for the front-leg version stays the same.

The rear-leg Low Angular Kick

Key points

- Do not move the upper body and *explode* into the movement.
- Keep your *guard up*.
- Just before impact, *inverse the rotation* direction of the hips.
- Always *follow up*.

Targets

The inside knee preferably. But also the outside knee, the side of the thighs and the upper ankles.

Typical Application

This is a very useful little Kick as an **attrition** move to the opponent's knees. As such, it is better done as a fast *front-leg* move, keeping your upper body immobile.
The Figures will show such an *Attrition Kick*, but followed by a very typical follow-up. This is probably the most useful classical use of this particular Kick: Use the **Angular Kick** to hit the inside knee of your opponent, *thus opening his legs*. Do not lower the leg, but, in an uninterrupted move, straighten the leg up along his thigh into a naturally developing *Front Groin Kick*. You can follow up by hitting his exposed back neck as he bends forward from the pain.

From his kicked knee, kick directly up into his groin

Specific training

The power of this Kick **can be greatly enhanced by thorough training**: practice on the standing heavy bag or on the upheld tire (See Figure). Drill for speed, for power and for no tell-tales. **Low Kicks require serious drilling!**
Overall kicking stamina will help a lot the power of "small" Kicks like this one. Methodical **PLYO –FLEX** training is warmly recommended.

Power drilling is essential to making this kick an effective one

Illustrative Photos

The Essential basic high Angular Front Kick

The Essential Outside Crescent Kick

18. THE FRONT PUSHING STOP-KICK TO KNEE-SCRAPE

General

This is a very interesting Kick, although anecdotic, and although very specifically to be used as a counter to a Spin-back Kick. It is basically a **Front Pushing Stop Kick** with a natural follow-up, and which I have discovered in *Wing Chun Kung Fu* practice. It is a bit esoteric, but extremely efficient when mastered and when used judiciously. As this work is aiming at being encyclopedic, it was important to record this variation's existence.

Description

The Figures show how to Front-stop-kick the buttock of your opponent as he spins back and as he starts lifting his leg for a Spin-back Hook Kick (in this example). As soon as you have connected, you start scraping down along his thigh, pushing down forcefully until you reach the back of his knee. You then Stomp down for a very painful and dangerous finish.

Specific training

- The Kick can only be seriously drilled *with a partner*. Practice the Stop Kick first, leaving your foot on his buttock (no chambering-back of the stop-kick!). Then start practicing the whole movement carefully.
- You can also practice the scraping down on a relatively light and pliable standing *bag* held by a partner.

19. THE FLYING STOMP KICK

General

This Kick could have been classified in future books under Flying Kicks or Suicide Kicks. We chose to place it here, because of the *stomping* angle. This is a very simple Kick to describe but acrobatic, unnecessarily dangerous to perform, and,- it should be said - a bit of a show-off. But it has been used very effectively in prominent MMA contests, where it has proved that it is definitely a worthwhile punishing maneuver. Like most spectacular kicks, it also has a great *psychological* effect on the opponent. In this case, it also has an overpowering physical side, which would make many opponents squirm.

Description

The Photos show how you jump high and lift your legs as high as possible in order to "fly" over your grounded opponent's guarding knees. You then land, with one foot beside his body, while the other **stomps** with *most of your body weight* onto anything in range: head, ribs, limbs,...
You can also, more dangerously, connect with *both feet* onto your opponent. You would probably fall yourself and have to roll to safety, but after an even more punishing stomp. Your choice.

A dangerous but intimidating and crushing Kick

Key points

If you chose to use this Kick, go all the way with full committment!
The dangers you need to be aware of when deciding to use this Kick are:

* You could be kicked in the groin while jumping up.
* You could lose your balance.

Specific training

- Practice (lightly) on a moving grounded *partner*, to learn to adjust for distance.
- Practice the *precision* of stomping by performing on a lying tire: one foot out of the tire, the second stomps a mark on the tire. You can simulate the obstacle of the opponent's leg with a lying heavy bag to jump over (Illustrated).

Drill on a tire; jump over a bag

- Drill for "*power*" on a lying focus pad, a lying bag or a lying tire.
- Practice *jumps* with airborne knee lifts in the air: Try to hit your pectorals, or even more, lift them outside your arms (See Photos).
- *Breaking* practice, eventually (*Tame Shiwari*). See Photos.
- And certainly: *Plyometric Exercises*!

High jumps for practice; arms outside

Jump and lift knees as high as possible; arms inside

A crushing Kick indeed

8.20 OTHER LOW KICKS

As mentioned at the beginning of this book, nearly all *Essential Kicks* can be delivered to the low gate, and hitherto become "Low Kicks". The kicks presented above in this book are especially suitable, or very specific to low delivery. We have also endeavored to use examples and applications to illustrate the specifics and the principles of low kicking. There are many more kicks and variations, and we have not presented here, for example, the specific Groin Kicks presented as **Essential Kicks** in our previous work. Some Essential Kicks are nearly only usable for groin attacks and could have been added here as Low Kicks. Just a few illustrative photos follow to whet the reader's appetite. Presenting here all the Essential Kicks executed at low heights would have been unnecessary repetitive work. The reader is invited to use common sense and to consult other work about basic kicks.

The Uppercut Hook Back Kick

The Outward Ghost Groin Kick

The Phantom Groin Kick

The Uppercut Back Kick

The Back Ghost Lift Kick

Recapitulating Table: Various Low Front Kicks

FRONT Low Kicks: *Soccer, Full Chamber, Inclined Soccer, Outside-tilted, Knee, Stomp, Groin*

AFTERWORD

We have come to the end of our study of the specifics of low kicking. As mentioned several times, there are many more Low Kicks variations and uses, be it as Stop Kicks, as Flying Kicks or as Ground Kicks, but categorization is very difficult for such a complex subject. Many Low Kicks and other applications are therefore presented in the other volumes of the 'Kicks' series.

The reader should remember that Low Kicks are often, when applicable, the best option for a fighter: they are stealthy, easy to execute, powerful, and generally aim at very sensitive targets (shins and groin). But, like everything else, they need serious and systematic drilling.

Low Kicks are ideal Cutting Stop Kicks – **Roy Faige** *on the author*

If there is anything at all that the author would like you to get out of reading this book, it is first and foremost that **Low Kicks require serious drilling**. Low Kicks often look simple and easy to execute; they are generally easier than their higher corresponding counterparts and require less flexibility. And therefore many fighters neglect the hard training they would invest in a 'normal' kick. This is a grave mistake! Avoiding the systematic and hard drilling of Low Kicks for power, speed, stealthiness and accuracy, will deprive a fighter of formidable weapons. Most Low Kicks delivered by conversant Martial artists will do some damage, even if they have not been drilled constantly. But this possible damage on impact can be easily doubled and trebled by an organized and permanent training program. Until the reader will do it and then use it in combat, he will have no idea of the deliverable power of the simplest and easiest of Low Kicks. It is simply incredible.

The author therefore implores the reader to give it a try and include Low kicks in his regular training routine. And remember:

If you fail to prepare, you're prepared to fail.
~Mark Spitz

The Low Kicks are also the Kicks the most suitable for a stealthy delivery, as they start low and stay low. The experienced Artist will make sure to avoid telegraphing his intentions and to keep his upper body immobile for as long as possible. The principles of Stealth are discussed in our book about 'Stealth Kicks' (where Low Kicks definitely star), and they should be applied at their maximum to any Low Kick the reader shall drill.

The importance of Low Kicks as 'Stop Kicks' will be further illustrated by the following excerpts from our book on the subject. Besides the classic Stop Kick illustrated many times here, there are nuanced near-stop-kicks that deserve the reader's attention:

1. _Attack on Preparation_: _Kicking before the attack can start_. This is the highest level of stop-kicking, the one every Martial Artist should strive for. Your opponent has decided to attack and basically has ordered his body to launch; you feel it and preempt it from even starting. To an outside observer, it may look like you are the aggressor. And any kick is relevant for this type of stop-kicking. It may read far-fetched, but every experienced Martial Artist knows how years of training hone the instincts and the ability to unconsciously "read" the opponent. This is the famous '**_Sen no sen_**' principle of the Japanese Martial Arts, touted, for example, by the famous swordsman _Miyamoto Musashi_. The Japanese high-level Artists even discern three different stages in the fraction of a second needed for a preemptive attack: "_Sakki_" (The ability to feel the decision of attack as it forms), "_Sen-no-sen_" (The decision of preempting the attack), and "_Senken_" (The start of the execution).

Stop Kick on preparation; it may seem as if you are the assailant

2. _Attack on completion_: _Kicking to catch the opponent at full extension of his attack._ this requires mastery of footwork and distance. You move the target,- your head or body-, away from the incoming attacking limb; if possible, just a few inches. And you develop your own counter so as to catch the opponent as he reaches full extension of his attack. The retreat or the evasion must be gradual and in tandem with the attack, in a way that unconsciously lets the opponent believe that he is going to connect (The '_Aiki_' spirit and principle). This kind of kick can be devastating, as an overextended opponent opens all his vital areas to the Stop Kick or Counter Kick.

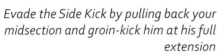

Evade the Side Kick by pulling back your midsection and groin-kick him at his full extension

3. Attack on recovery: *Kicking to catch the opponent as he swings back into original position after an unsuccessful attack.* You evade just enough as in the previous type, and then attack as he retreats back to his original fighting stance.

Front Kick on recovery from a rear-leg Penetrating Front Kick

Low Kick on recovery from a Roundhouse Kick attack

An important last distinction to make is the following: All Stop Kicks can be used in an **offensive** manner *by drawing the attacker into a specific attack.* This is valid for all Stop Kick types. This is the 4th principle, of "***Attack by Drawing***": You open your guard or place yourself in such a way, that the opponent will see an opening beckoning him for a (more or less) specific attack. As soon as you feel his attack taking form, you will stop-kick him. This is more of a tactical distinction, but it differentiates between "real" *defensive* Stop Kicks and offensive "*Drawing*" Stop Kicks.

And Please remember that the fact that our Book Series has cataloged a great number of Kicks does not mean that you have to know and master them all. As already mentioned, a good Martial Artist must first master the basics of his chosen style by hard work on the Essential techniques. Only when he has done so, should he try advanced maneuvers and special techniques from other Arts. He should then drill new and unconventional techniques, and then try them in free fighting. A real Artist will then know how to choose only a few techniques that are suitable to his morphology, psychology and liking. These very few techniques will then have to be drilled for thousands and thousands of times until they become natural. During the fight, it is the body that intuitively choses the best technique to be used. If you have to think about what to do, you have already lost! The expected relevant quote follows:

I fear not the man who has practiced 10,000 kicks once, but I fear the man who has practiced one kick 10,000 times.
~ Bruce Lee

I am not sorry to nag, and I will conclude with a last reminder: **LOW KICKS REQUIRE SERIOUS DRILLING, AND THE RESULTS WILL BE AMAZING**. Even the most cynical will be surprised.

Therefore, get to work; and remember:

Pain is the best instructor, but no one wants to go to his class.
~Choi, Hong Hi, Founder of Taekwon-Do

<u>If you have enjoyed the book and appreciate the effort behind this series, you are invited to write a short honest review on Amazon.com</u>...It has become extremely difficult to promote one's work in this day and age, and your support would be much appreciated. Thanks!

All questions, comments, additional techniques, special or vintage Photos about Suicide Kicks, or other Kicks, are welcomed by the author and would be introduced with credit in future editions. Just email:**martialartkicks@gmail.com**

The author is trying to build a complete series of work that, once finished, could become an encyclopedic base of the whole of the Martial Arts-Kicking realm, a base on which others could build and add their own experiences.

In his endeavors the author has already penned:

- **The Essential Book of Martial Arts Kicks** – *Tuttle Publishing* (2010)
- **Plyo-Flex** - Training for Explosive Martial Arts Kicks (2013)
- **Low Kicks** - Advanced Martial Arts Kicks for Attacking the Lower Gates (2013)
- **Stop Kicks** – Jamming, Obstructing, Stopping, Impaling, Cutting and Preemptive Kicks (2014)
- **Ground Kicks** – Advanced Martial Arts Kicks for groundfighting (2015)
- **Stealth Kicks** - The Forgotten Art of Ghost Kicking (2015)
- **Sacrifice Kicks** - Flying, Hopping, Jumping and Suicide Kicks (2016)

In the same frame of mind, the following works are in preparation:

- Combo Kicks
- Krav Maga Kicks
- Joint Kicks

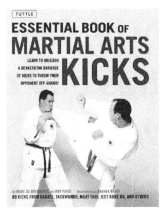

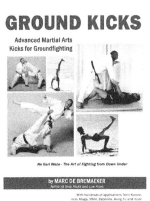
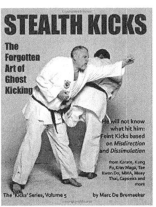

Only one who devotes himself to a cause with his whole strength and soul can be a true master. For this reason mastery demands all of a person.
~Albert Einstein

Sacrifice Kicks will comprehensively present the most important Martial Arts Airborne Kicks: Flying Kicks, Hopping Kicks, Jumping Kicks and Suicide Kicks. They have been dubbed 'Sacrifice' in the spirit of Judo's redoubtable Sutemi Takedowns in which one sacrifices his balance in order to throw his opponent down. Flying Kicks are not about showmanship, they are very effective techniques when used judiciously. They need not be necessarily high and spectacular; they can be surprising Hopping Kicks executed long and low. And Suicide Kicks take the Sacrifice principles a little further: they are extremely unexpected techniques delivered airborne, but with little hope of landing on one's feet, unlike classic Flying Kicks. Over 1000 Photos and Illustrations will help you develop your airborne kicking skills, regardless of your personal style.

Plyometrics and Flexibility Training for Explosive Martial Arts Kicks and Performance Sports Plyo-Flex is a system of plyometric exercises and intensive flexibility training designed to increase your kicking power, speed, flexibility and skill level. Based on scientific principles, Plyo-Flex exercises will boost your muscles, joints and nervous system interfaces to the next performance level. After only a few weeks of training, you should see a marked improvement in the speed of your kicks and footwork, the power of your kicks, the height of your jumps, your stamina and your overall flexibility. Hundreds of illustrations and photographs will guide you through the basic plyometric and stretching exercises. Once you've mastered the basics, add the kicking-oriented variations to your workout for an extra challenge.

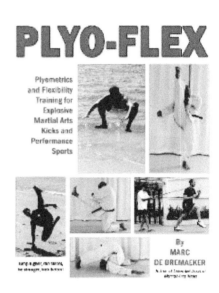

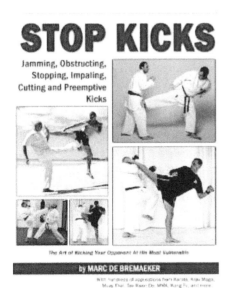

Stop Kicks are among the most effective, sophisticated kicks a fighter can use. And because they hit your opponent at his most vulnerable, they are also the safest way to pre-empt or counter an attack. Stop Kicks are delivered just as your opponent is fully committed to an attack, physically or mentally, meaning it is too late for him to change his mind. Hitting an opponent in mid-attack gives you the added advantage of using his attacking momentum against him. Stop Kicks: Jamming, Obstructing, Stopping, Impaling, Cutting and Preemptive Kicks presents a well organized array of stop-kicking techniques from a wide range of martial arts. Learn Pushing Kicks, Timing Kicks, Cutting Kicks, Obstruction Kicks, and Block Kicks from the hard-hitting styles of Muay Thai, Karatedo, Krav Maga, Tae Kwon Do, MMA and more.

Whether you are on the ground by choice or you have been taken down, whether your opponent is standing or is on the ground with you, whether you are a good grappler or you are trying to keep a good grappler at bay, whether you were caught unawares sitting on the floor or you have evaded down on purpose, whether you are a beginner or an experienced martial artist...this book has the right kick for the situation. In **Ground Kicks**: Advanced Martial Arts Kicks for Ground-fighting from Karate, Krav Maga, MMA, Capoeira, Kung Fu and more, Marc De Bremaeker has created a comprehensive collection of Ground Kicks, with hundreds of applications for sport fighting and self-defense situation. Packed with over 1200 photographs and illustrations, Ground Kicks also includes specific training tips for practicing each kick effectively.

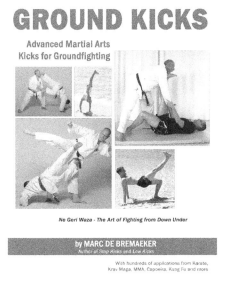

GROUND KICKS
Advanced Martial Arts Kicks for Groundfighting

Ne Geri Waza - The Art of Fighting from Down Under

by MARC DE BREMAEKER
Author of Stop Kicks and Low Kicks

With hundreds of applications from Karate, Krav Maga, MMA, Capoeira, Kung Fu and more

STEALTH KICKS
The Forgotten Art of Ghost Kicking

He will not know what hit him: Feint Kicks based on *Misdirection* and *Dissimulation*

from Karate, Kung Fu, Krav Maga, Tae Kwon Do, MMA, Muay Thai, Capoeira and more

The 'Kicks' Series, Volume 5   by Marc De Bremaeker

Stealth Kicks will introduce you to the Art of executing Kicks that your opponent will not see coming. This subject has never been treated comprehensively before. Whether you are a beginner or an experienced Artist, you will find suitable Kicks or tips to modify your current techniques to give them stealth. It will help you to score in Sport confrontations or make sure to come on top in real life Self-Defense situations. The *Feint Kicks* presented are based on misdirection: they will aim at provoking a misguided reaction that will open your adversary to the real kick intended. The *Ghost Kicks* presented are based on dissimulation and will travel out of your opponent's range of vision to catch him unawares.
Together with general feinting techniques and specific training tips, hundreds of applications will introduce you to the sneaky Art of stealth kicking and will make you a better and unpredictable fighter. Crammed with over 2300 photos and drawings for an easy understanding of the concept of Stealth.

Perfection is not attainable, but if we chase perfection we can catch excellence.
~Vince Lombardi

OTHER GENRES FROM FONS SAPIENTIAE

AVAILABLE IN PAPERBACK AND KINDLE FORMATS ON AMAZON

The Manual is the definitive guide to Enhanced Concentration, Super Memory, Speed Reading, Note-Taking, Rapid Mental Arithmetic, and the *Ultimate Study Method* (USM).

The techniques presented are the culmination of decades of practical experience combined with the latest scientific research and time-tested practices. The system described herewith will allow the practitioner to:

• Read faster with higher comprehension.
• Remember any type of information instantly.
• Store information in long-term memory.
• Enhance concentration and focus.
• Access deeper levels of the mind.
• Induce relaxation.
• Rapidly perform complex mental arithmetic.
• Master the Ultimate Study Method (USM).

USM is a synergistic combination of established techniques for Concentration, Long-Term Memory, Speed Reading, and Note-Taking. It involves a systematic procedure that allows the practitioner to study any topic fast, efficiently and effectively. USM can be applied to all areas of educational study, academic research, business endeavours, as well as professional life in general.

Rain Fund: A riveting thriller

"...For the safety of the readers, this book ought to come with the disclaimer: leave this book read half-way at your own risk. Unless you are Superman, you won't be able to concentrate on much else until you have read the last page of "Rain Fund". The time has come for Patterson, Ludlum, Dan Brown et al to slide over and make space at the top for Marc Brem." - Shweta Shankar for Readers' Favorite

"...In the good tradition of Ludlum and Grisham. Five Stars" Aldo Levy

"Autistic geniuses charting financial markets; Mobster-fuelled Ponzi schemes; sophisticated hardware viruses; spies; and a rising superpower that strives for dominance – so realistic it is frightening."

Coming Soon !

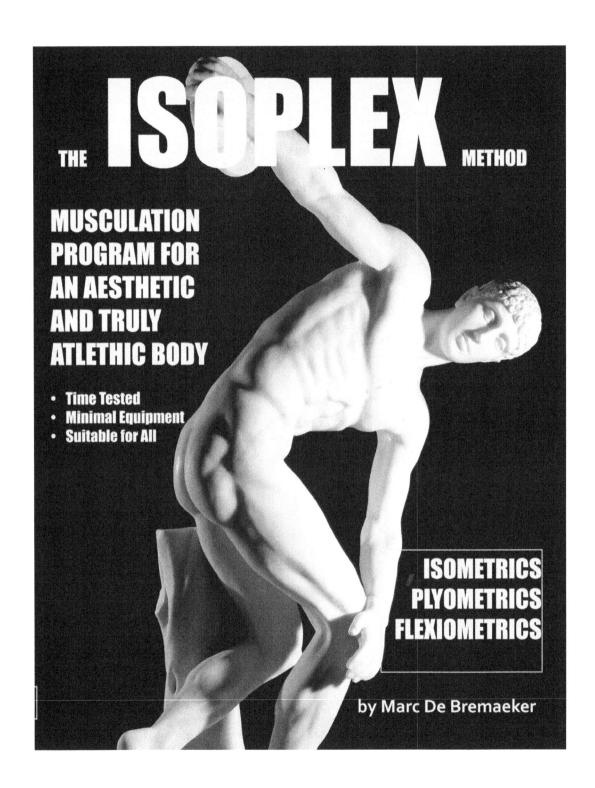

Use only that which works, and take it from any place you can find it.
~Bruce Lee

LOW KICKS

Made in the USA
Las Vegas, NV
17 December 2021

37976829R00092